THE PUFFIN BOOK OF
1000 FUN FACTS

The Puffin
BOOK
~ of ~
1000
FUN
FACTS

PUFFIN BOOKS

An imprint of Penguin Random House

PUFFIN BOOKS

USA | Canada | UK | Ireland | Australia
New Zealand | India | South Africa | China | Singapore

Puffin Books is part of the Penguin Random House group of companies
whose addresses can be found at global.penguinrandomhouse.com

Published by Penguin Random House India Pvt. Ltd
4th Floor, Capital Tower 1, MG Road,
Gurugram 122 002, Haryana, India

Penguin
Random House
India

First published in Puffi n by Penguin Books India 2013

Text and illustrations copyright © Penguin Books India 2013

Content researched and developed by excalibEr Solutions

10 9 8 7 6 5 4 3 2

ISBN 9780143332336

Typeset in Gotham Book by R. Ajith Kumar, New Delhi
Printed at Manipal Technologies Limited, India

www.penguin.co.in

MIX
Paper | Supporting
responsible forestry
FSC® C043100

This is a legitimate digitally printed version of the book and therefore might not
have certain extra finishing on the cover.

CONTENTS

INDIA

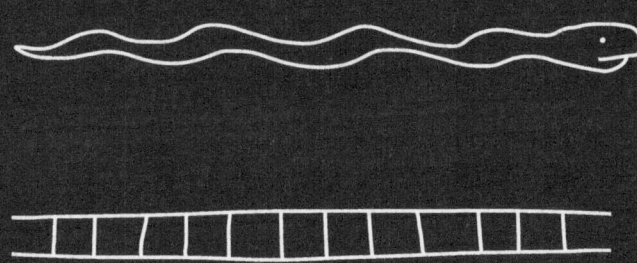

1

Saint Gyandev invented the board game
'Snakes and Ladders' in the 13th century.
He called it 'Mokshapat', in which the ladders
symbolized virtues and the snakes
represented vices.

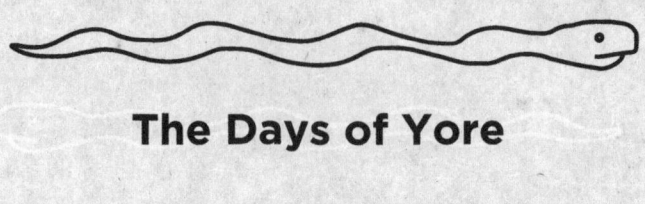

The Days of Yore

2. Through the ages, India has gone through multiple conquests and invasions. But India has never invaded any country in its entire history!

3. It was the Mughals who ruled India for the longest time. Can you believe that for nearly 200 years (1526–1707), an unbroken succession of Mughal emperors ascended the throne of India?

4. Diamonds were first discovered in India, in the Golconda riverbeds, 4000 years ago. In fact, India was the only source of diamonds in the world until 1896!

5. Did you know that badminton originated in India and that it was initially called 'Poona'? When the Duke of Beaufort learnt the game and introduced it in England, the Englishmen found the name weird and were reluctant to play it. The Duke renamed it 'badminton', after the name of an estate he owned, and the game caught on!

6. Around 600 BCE, criminals would get their noses chopped off as punishment. The skin from their foreheads was taken to reconstruct their damaged noses. Now we know how plastic surgeries were done in ancient India!

7. Four major religions originated in India—Hinduism, Jainism, Sikhism and Buddhism. 25 per cent of the world's population follows one of these religions even today!

8. The Iron Pillar in Delhi stands testimony to the artistry of ancient Indian blacksmiths. The pillar has withstood corrosion for 1600 years!

9. Did you know that cotton was first spun and woven in India? The Mughals referred to the fabric as 'the cloth of running water' or 'morning dew'.

10. The first woman leader of India, Razia Sultana (1205–1240), ruled only for three years, and was murdered soon after.

11. During the Vedic era, the sovereignty of a king was marked by the sacrifice of a horse.

12. The knowledge system that existed in ancient India, known as the Chaturdasha Vidya, had 14 disciplines, divided into three broad categories—the Vedas, the Vedangas and the Upangas.

13. Did you know that the world's first university was established in India? Takshila University, established in 700 BCE, taught about 60 subjects to more than 10,000 students from all over the world. The University of Nalanda, another reputed educational institution in India, was established in the 5th century.

14. Artists trained in the Kangra school of art would use strange substances to paint, like blood and crushed beetles, and their brushes were often made of a single hair!

15. One of the earliest schools of medicine known to mankind is Ayurveda. It was consolidated by Charaka (considered the 'father of medicine') nearly 2500 years ago!

16. How complicated is it to treat urinary stones, fractures or cataracts? How challenging is it to perform brain surgeries, caesareans and cosmetic surgeries? With the advancements in the field of medicine today, these procedures aren't very difficult any more. But did you know that Sushruta, the 'father

INDIA

3

of surgery', used to conduct these complicated procedures 2600 years ago without all the sophistication we have today?

17. Ancient Indian medicine was quite advanced for its times, which is proved by the fact that anatomy, aetiology (study of the causes of diseases), physiology, genetics, immunity, digestion, metabolism and the usage of anaesthesia are mentioned in the ancient texts of India.

18. The first successful eye transplant (corneal transplant) was performed in India. It was done by a British army surgeon who restored his pet antelope's vision by taking the cornea of a recently killed antelope.

19. Though the technique of acupuncture was perfected in China, it originated in India 3000 years ago. On the other hand, homeopathy originated in Germany, though most of the practitioners are from India.

20. The art of hypnotism was evolved by Abade Faria, a Goan priest. His statue stands in Panjim. This Goan has been immortalized in the classic novel *The Count of Monte Cristo*, written by Alexander Dumas.

21. Aryabhata, the famous Indian mathematician and astronomer, invented the zero. To honour his invaluable contributions to the field of astronomy, a crater in the moon has been named after him. In fact, the first satellite launched by India was also named after him.

22. Arabic numerals were not invented in Arabia. They were invented in India.

23. The decimal number system and the 'place value system' in mathematics were developed in India as early as 100 BCE.

24. Calculus, trigonometry and algebra originated in India.

25. The Indian mathematician Budhayana calculated the value of 'pi' and also explained the Pythagorean Theorem in the 6th century. Sridharacharya, another Indian mathematician, used quadratic equations in the 11th century.

26. While the largest number used by the Greeks and the Romans was just 106, Indians used numbers as large as 10^{53} during the Vedic age (5000 BCE).

27. India derives its name from the river Indus. The valleys around this river were home to the earliest settlers of the country. The Aryans referred to the Indus as Sindhu, and the Persians converted the name to Hindu once they invaded the country. The words 'Hindu' and 'Sindhu' were combined to form 'Hindustan' (which translates to 'land of Hindus'). But the official Sanskrit name of India is Bharat, and that was how it was referred to during the Golden Age (Satya Yuga).

28. Sanskrit is said to be the mother of all languages. In fact, it is the only language that has a precise syntax and grammar and hence, suitable for developing computer software!

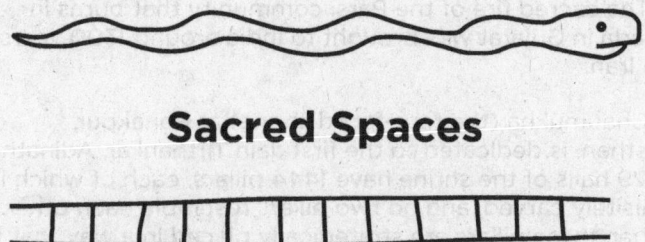

Sacred Spaces

29. Many South Indian temples are famous for their musical stone pillars. A single pillar is chiselled into seven to 16 bars. When you tap the bars with a wooden mallet, you can hear distinct notes, just like from a xylophone.

30. The Brihadeswara temple in Thanjavur, Tamil Nadu, is the world's first granite temple. The shikhara or the rising tower is made from a single 80-tonne block of granite rock. This temple was built during the reign of Rajaraja Chola in just five years (between 1004 CE and 1009 CE).

31. The Rameshwaram temple in Tamil Nadu has one of the longest corridors in the world (4000 feet in length), with 985 richly carved pillars on both sides.

32. One of the world's oldest rock forts is in Tiruchirappalli, Tamil Nadu. This hill fort, constructed on a 273-feet-high rock, was built billions of years ago. In fact, Tiruchirappalli also has the world's oldest surviving dam—Kallanai. Built during the Chola rule, it stretches to about 24 km across the river Kaveri.

33. A simple handclap at the entrance of the Golconda Fort near Hyderabad, which is 400 feet below the topmost pavilion, can be heard clearly by a person standing at the top!

34. The Kailash temple at Ellora, Aurangabad, was excavated after 20,000 tonnes of rock were chiselled out. There was no mechanical aid to carry out this tedious project. Apparently, the whole temple was carved out of a single hill and created by digging a 30-metre-deep trench on all three sides, leaving just a block of rock for the temple.

35. The sacred fire of the Parsi community that burns in Udwada in Gujarat was brought to India around 1300 years ago from Iran.

36. Chaumukha (the four-faced shrine) at Ranakpur, Rajasthan, is dedicated to the first Jain Tirthankar, Adinath. The 29 halls of the shrine have 1444 pillars, each of which is exquisitely carved, and no two pillars resemble each other. Further, these pillars are strategically placed in a way that the view of the deity is unobstructed from anywhere.

37. The Se Cathedral in Goa has an unusual bell. Its din can be heard nearly 14 km away at Panjim! But weirdly enough, a person standing right next to the bell only hears a soothing, melodious sound.

38. Until about 2000 years ago, the Buddha was never represented as a human. The first human form of the Buddha was carved in Mathura, Uttar Pradesh.

39. Do you consider rats pests? The pilgrims of the Karni Devi temple near Bikaner, Rajasthan, regard them as *kabas* or children and worship the rats as the descendants of the deity!

40. The construction of the Somnath Shiva temple in Gujarat is such that there is no land between it and the South Pole.

41. The largest natural cave in the Himalayas is situated at a height of 12,729 feet. It is a major attraction for tourists, especially during the months of July and August, when a 'shiva linga' of pure ice gets naturally formed. A clear explanation about how it is formed is still not known. It is believed that the linga waxes and wanes depending on the full moon or the new moon phases.

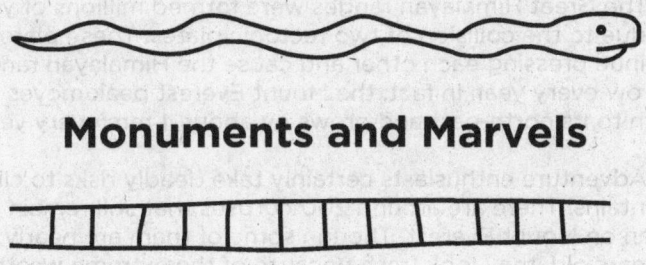

Monuments and Marvels

42. A 1000 elephants carried the material required to build the Taj Mahal from various parts of India to the construction site.

43. The 72.5-metre-high Qutub Minar, situated in Delhi, is the world's tallest free-standing brick minaret. This marvellous UNESCO World Heritage Site consists of five distinct storeys, with 379 stairs leading to the top.

44. The Bhimbetka rock shelters in Madhya Pradesh are home to some of the earliest known prehistoric paintings of the world. Painted with natural colours, vegetable dyes, roots and animal fat, these beautiful pictures have not faded over time, even though they are almost 12,000 years old!

45. Dholavira, a prominent archaeological site in Gujarat, dates back to the Indus Valley Civilization and is the fifth largest Harappan site. This region had one of the earliest sophisticated water conservation channels in the world. The reservoir was used for storing fresh rainwater.

46. Is there a Great Wall in India as in China? The answer is YES! The wall is in the Aravalli hills in Rajasthan. It has around 32 fortresses, and was built by Rana Kumbha, a medieval Rajput ruler.

47. Mandu, the largest fortified city in India during the medieval era, has a swinging palace called the Hindola Mahal. The sloping side walls have a peculiar design that creates an illusion that the entire structure is swaying!

48. The Great Himalayan ranges were formed millions of years ago due to the collision of two tectonic plates. These plates continue pressing each other and cause the Himalayan ranges to grow every year. In fact, the Mount Everest peak moves by 10 cm to its north-east and grows by about 4 mm every year.

49. Adventure enthusiasts certainly take deadly risks to climb mountains. There are around 200 corpses that still remain frozen on Mount Everest. Though some of them are nearly 50 years old, they look fresh because of the extreme weather conditions. Mountaineers can see these corpses as they make their way up. The death zone begins nearly 26,000 feet above sea level, where the air is so thin that the slightest mistake can result in frostbite or death!

50. Siachen Glacier, located in the eastern Karakoram Range in the Himalayas in Jammu and Kashmir, is the northernmost point of India. The world's highest public telephone booth is located here.

51. The highest bridge in the world was constructed by the Indian Army between the Suru and the Drass rivers in the Himalayas in the year 1982.

52. The largest river island in India is Majula, situated in Assam on the river Brahmaputra. The island was formed due to the turbulence of the river and its tributaries, mainly the Lohit. There is a threat of the whole island being washed away every year. Heedless of this fact, a population of nearly 1.5 lakh people still continues to live there, spread over 23 villages.

53. The Sundarbans, the largest delta in the world, span two countries—India and Bangladesh—and are formed by the rivers Brahmaputra, Ganga and Meghana. Covering 54 islands, this saltwater swamp is known for its mangroves and Sundari trees.

54. The state of Rajasthan has two distinct geographical regions—desert in the west and forest in the east. The Aravallis separate these two regions.

55. Do you know that the horse-shoe-shaped Chitrakoot waterfall, formed by the Indravati river, is called the Niagara Falls of India? The width of this 100-feet-high waterfall can be as much as 1000 feet between July and October, after the monsoons.

56. Khur, the Indian wild ass, is found only in Rann of Kutch, the salt desert in Gujarat. The speed of the animal is such that a relay of horses is needed to tire the ass before it's finally caught!

57. There is a 'cobra village' called Shetphal in Sholapur, Maharashtra. Each house in the village provides a resting place for cobras in the ceiling rafts! Interestingly, no person has died of a cobra bite in the village till now. The snakes live in their houses like pets!

58. The New Subzi Mandi at Azadpur, Delhi, is Asia's largest fruit and vegetable wholesale market, providing a flourishing business to nearly 30,000 vendors!

59. The Jantar Mantar in Delhi has two special pillars, 12 feet high and set 17 feet apart. These pillars represent the shortest and the longest days of the year (21 December and 21 June, respectively). On the 21st of December, the southern pillar casts a shadow on the northern pillar and covers it entirely. On the 21st of June, no shadow is observed on the northern pillar.

60. The village of Pandhurna celebrates a unique festival every year called Gotmar in the month of September. The word Gotmar means 'beating with small stones'. A tree trunk with a flag tied on top is placed in the middle of the river that flows through the village. People from Pandhurna and Savargao, the neighbouring village, gather on either side of the river and start pulling the flag. Each side tries to prevent the other from pulling the flag by throwing rocks or stones. It is no surprise that this weird custom results in injuries and deaths every year!

61. The Kumbh Mela, which is also known as the Grand Pitcher Festival, takes place once every 12 years. In 2001, nearly 60 million people attended this festival, and it broke the record of the world's biggest gathering. An aerial photograph of this was captured by a satellite in space!

62. The Lotus Temple in Delhi, one of the most visited temples in the world, welcomes almost 50 million visitors annually. The 27 gigantic petals of the lotus-shaped temple are covered in marble.

63. One of the main attractions of Kochi, Kerala, is the sight of fish-catching with Cheena vala (Chinese fishing nets), which are made of bamboo and teak frames. Visitors can take a boat tour in the harbour or watch this interesting activity from the northern end of Vasco-da-Gama Square. Sadly, the practice is fast vanishing as these nets ask for huge maintenance and operational costs. Only a dozen of them are in use now.

64. Situated in Arunachal Pradesh at an altitude of nearly 10,000 feet above sea level, the 330-year-old Tawang Monastery, the largest Buddhist monastery in India, is the second largest monastery in Asia.

Famous Folk

65. The wardrobe of the sixth Nizam of Hyderabad, Mir Mahbub Ali Khan (Mahbub Ali Pasha), was a 176-feet-long corridor with cupboards on either side. He never wore the same clothes twice in his life!

66. Bhaskaracharya, the famous Indian astronomer and mathematician, calculated the exact time taken by the earth to complete its orbit around the sun as early as in the 5th century. The value given by him was 365.258756484 days.

67. It was Akbar who made political unification of North India possible. Before this, non-Muslims had to pay poll tax (jizya) to live in a land inhabited by Muslims, and Hindus had to pay pilgrimage tax. Both these taxes were abolished after Akbar married women from Hindu families and included Hindus in his court.

68. Can you imagine a person gobbling up 200 earthworms, each measuring 10 cm, in 30 seconds? Well, this record is held by an Indian, popularly known as 'Snake Manoharan'. What a way to get your daily dose of protein!

Movie Mania!

69. The ever flourishing entertainment industry in India brings out nearly 800 movies every year. More than 3 billion movie tickets are sold in India every year!

70. We all know that Mahatma Gandhi had a huge number of loyal followers while he was alive. But very few people can command such loyalty even after death. When the movie *Gandhi* was shot, 3,00,000 extras were present at the shooting spot for the funeral scene. Out of these, only

1,00,000 were paid a very nominal fee for their appearance. The rest did it for free!

Holy Cow!

71. Do you know that India has the most number of mosques in the world? The total number is nearly 3,00,000!

72. India has the largest postal network in the world—with over 1,50,000 post offices.

73. The number of newborns every year in India is much more than the entire population of Australia.

74. The Tirupati temple in Tamil Nadu is the richest temple in the world.

75. The centuries-old caste system in India still has serious repercussions. Only a few decades ago, when a bus fell into a river just outside New Delhi, the passengers refused to share a rope and climb to safety, simply because they all belonged to different castes. Needless to say, they all drowned.

76. The tribal groups of Nagaland are collectively called the Nagas. There are around 16 different tribal communities recognized by the state. How do they distinguish between the various tribes? Well, they are identified by the kind of shawls they use. The different designs and colours on the shawls indicate the community and the social status of the wearer.

77. India produces a 1000 varieties of mangoes. Each of these varieties is named after colours, places, shapes, tastes, flavours, precious stones and even royalty.

78. People who follow Zoroastrianism in India do not bury the dead, to avoid polluting the natural elements (air, water, fire and earth). Instead, they leave the bodies in buildings where vultures can feed on them. These buildings are called Towers of Silence. Once the bones dry, they are collected and swept into a central well.

79. Did you know that the national bird of India, the peacock, was initially bred for food?

80. Can you believe that only around 1300 Royal Bengal tigers are alive in India now?

81. Do you know that the self-renewing Indian fig tree or the banyan tree is the national tree of India and represents immortality?

82. Have you seen marigold flowers being used in Hindu marriages? They are considered auspicious as they are said to be symbols of happiness, prosperity and good fortune.

83. India is the largest milk producing country in the world.

84. India has the third largest road network in the world. It covers nearly 2 million miles!

85. India is the leading exporter of bananas and the largest producer of chickpeas and kidney beans.

86. India experiences six seasons every year—summer monsoon, summer, winter monsoon, winter, autumn and spring.

87. The most popular beverage in India is tea. In fact, India is the world's largest producer of tea, along with China.

88. It isn't uncommon to see tourists being harassed by monkeys at various places. The authorities at Chittorgarh railway station in Rajasthan have come up with a way of outsourcing the job of evicting the monkeys there. They have announced a cash prize for the person who outwits at least 15 monkeys and succeeds in sending them to a far-off place, never to return to the station. Are you ready to participate in this competition?

89. What is the worth of the most expensive attire in your wardrobe? A businessman in Pune became the talk of the town after he bought a gold shirt worth 1.27 crores, weighing more than 3 kg. The shirt was crafted by 15 goldsmiths who worked more than 15 hours every day for close to 15 days!

90. Can you imagine buying a new car, banging it and dumping it after using it just once? This is what a Haryana-based businessman did one day, and that too with a brand new Mercedes Benz! What on earth could be the explanation for such bizarre behaviour?

91. India shares its independence day with South Korea, Bahrain and Congo.

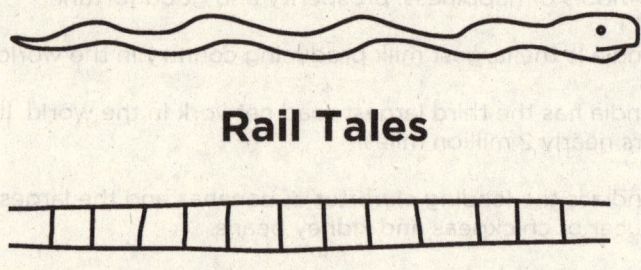

Rail Tales

92

- The largest single organization to employ the most number of people in the world is the Indian Railways network. It gives job opportunities to nearly 1.5 million people!

- Special trains are often run by the organization, satisfying some peculiar requirements. There is a 'Fish Therapy Special' that runs every year from Guwahati to Hyderabad, catering specifically to asthma patients. Patients are made to swallow a live Murral fish that is medicated once they reach Hyderabad.

- What could be the longest station name on the Indian Railways? It is Venkatanarasimharajuvaripeta!

- Porters are commonly seen in Indian railway stations. But have you seen women working as porters in India? The Bhavnagar railway station in Gujarat is the only station where you can see women porters.

AROUND THE WORLD

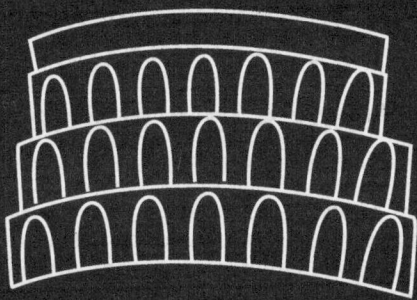

93

The Colosseum in Rome could accommodate nearly 50,000 spectators at a time, and was used for about 400 years before it was damaged by stone robbers and natural disasters. The Colosseum was where gladiatorial contests and dramatic performances, not to mention human executions and animal hunts, were held before the medieval era. The Italian counterpart of the 5-cent euro coin depicts this Roman architectural masterpiece.

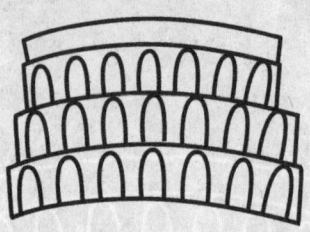

What's in a Name?

94. The longest place name in an English-speaking country is Taumatawhakatangihangakoauauotamateaturipukakapiki-maungahoronukupokaiwhenuakitanatahu, the Maori name of a hill in New Zealand. Consisting of 85 characters, this name has been recorded in the *Guinness Book of World Records* and is still in use.

95. The longest place name in Europe is a village named Lanfairpwllgwyngyllgogerychwyrndrobwllllantysiliogogogoch. The village is on Anglesey Island, in Wales.

The name has garnered lot of tourist attraction. In fact, visitors from all over the world stop at the village railway station to take pictures of the signboard.

LLANFAIRPWLLGWYNGYLLGOGERYCHWYRNDROBWLLLLANTYSILIOGOGOGOCH
ST MARY'S CHURCH IN THE HOLLOW OF THE WHITE HAZEL NEAR TO THE RAPID WHIRLPOOL OF LLANTYSILLIO OF THE RED CAVE

96. The largest natural lake in Massachusetts is called Long Pond, situated in Lakeville. Webster Lake, consisting of a shoreline of nearly 27 km, is situated near the border of Connecticut. It is the second largest natural lake in Massachusetts and is spring-fed. Interestingly, the official name of this lake is a 45-letter word: Lake Chargoggagoggmanchauggagoggchaubunagungamaugg. This is the longest place name in the United States. According to the Algonquian languages (spoken by Native Americans), the name means 'Fishing Place at the Boundaries—Neutral Meeting Grounds'.

97. In Texas, there is a town named Ding Dong, which had a population of just 22 people in the year 1990. There is an interesting story about how this town got its name. Zulis Bell and Bert Bell, who were the earliest settlers here, ran a store. While designing the signboard for it, the artist, Cohn Cohen Hoover painted two bells and wrote the initials of the two brothers inside them. Below the bells, he wrote the words 'Ding' and 'Dong'. Now the community living here is called the 'Ding Dong' community!

98. Have you noticed that the names of all the continents—Asia, Africa, Antarctica, Australia, America (North and South) and Europe—start and end with the same letter? Similarly, all states in the US that begin with 'A' end with the same letter except for Arkansas.

99. There are about 10 towns in the US named Hollywood!

100. There is a city called Rome in every continent in the world!

101. Streets in Japan don't have any names.

102. 'Canada' is actually an aboriginal word and translates to 'Big Village'. Bonus fact: There are more lakes in Canada than the combined number of lakes in the rest of the world.

103. Do you know how Venezuela got its name? The explorers who discovered it were reminded of Venice and hence called it 'Little Venice'. This was later translated into Spanish as Venezuela.

104. The capital of South Korea, Seoul, translates to just that—'the capital'—in Korean.

105. Do you know that Spain means 'the land of rabbits'?

106. The full name of Los Angeles is El Pueblo de Nuestra Senora la Reina de los Angeles de Porciuncula!

107. Can you send postcards to Paradise and Hell? Yes, you can! These two towns, Paradise and Hell, are situated in Michigan. Another 'Hell' exists in Cayman Islands. In fact, a gift shop at this place greets you with a board saying 'Welcome to Hell'!

108. The *Guinness Book of World Records* had listed a town named 6 (in West Virginia) as the shortest place name. After the name was spelt out as 'Six', it was removed from the list. Now, the shortest name is really simple to remember—it's just 'Y' and it's in Alaska!

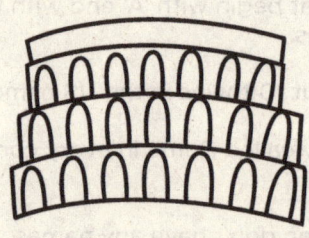

Show and Tell

109. Netherlands has the most number of museums in the world. Do you know that there are over 50 museums only in Amsterdam?

110. Ever heard of a museum dedicated to spoons? A museum in New Jersey has a display of around 5000 spoons from almost every country and state in the world!

111. Can you believe that there are more than 4000 varieties of prepared mustards all over the world? If you want to see them, visit the Mount Horeb Mustard Museum in Wisconsin.

112. There is a museum dedicated to just strawberries! It is called Musée de la Fraise and is situated on the banks of the river Meuse. This five-room exhibition presents the rich culture and history of strawberries grown in the region.

113. Have you ever heard of museums dedicated to just popcorn? There are only two of them in the world and they are both in the state of Ohio. The Wyandot Popcorn Museum has one of the largest collections of popcorn antiques that have been restored by skilled craftsmen. Two of the displayed antiques in the museum are more than a 100 years old. The other museum, the J.H. Fentress Antique popcorn Museum, showcases 35 Butter-Kist popcorn machines in addition to old popcorn boxes, tins and bags.

114. The American Kennel Club Museum in Missouri displays art collections dedicated only to dogs. The displays in the museum consist of paintings, drawings, sculptures, porcelain and bronze decorative pieces.

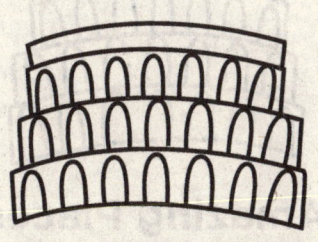

'Grave' Matters

115. The San Francisco City and County, occupying just about 49 square miles, had quite a few cemeteries in the past. However, during the early 1900s, the population grew and land became scarce. Around 1940, only two cemeteries (Presidio and Mission Dolores) and one crematorium (named Columbarium) remained. Currently, excluding the federal National Cemetery at Lincoln Way, there are no cemeteries in San Francisco!

116. The dead to living person ratio in the 'Cemetery Town', Colma, California, is 750 to 1! That's because San Francisco City was forced to outlaw burials in 1902 due to apprehensions about public health and absence of space, following which Colma was established 5 miles south of San Francisco just to entomb the deceased!

117. In 1785, the city of Paris adopted an innovative method to make room in the cemeteries for new dead bodies. How, you ask? Easy, by removing the bones of those who were dead and buried there before! These bones were taken and stacked up in tunnels now known as catacombs.

118. Can a cemetery be a tourist spot? Cimetière du Père-Lachaise, located in Paris, certainly is. What do you think attracts people to this location? Well, famous personalities from all over the world are buried here. You can find all kinds of legends from musicians and artists to sculptors and authors, all in one place.

Amazing Places

119. Indonesia has 13,600 islands!

120. Only 2 per cent of the Caribbean Islands has been inhabited. The rest is still unexplored, and occupied by exotic flora and fauna.

121. Contrary to popular belief, the Canary Islands were not named after the birds; they were named after a breed of wild dogs! In fact, when explorers visited these islands during the 16th century, they brought to the place pretty birds that sang, and they named these birds 'canaries' after the islands' name!

122. The longest street in the world is in Canada and connects Lake Ontario (Toronto) and Lake Simcoe (that leads to the Upper Great Lakes). Covering about 1896 km, the street is referred to as 'Main Street Ontario' or 'Yonge Street' (pronounced as 'Young').

123. The richest source of mineral sands in the world is present in the smallest of the five continents—Australia.

124. The only state bordered by rivers on the east and the west is Iowa. While Mississippi occupies its east, Big Sioux and Missouri are situated to its west.

125. The only freshwater sharks in the world are found in Lake Nicaragua, the largest lake in Central America.

126. Can a city be located in two continents? Istanbul is—it bridges Asia and Europe.

127. Singapore, one of the most urbanized countries in the world, has only one train station! More than half the country is still covered in greenery.

128. The Mall of America employs more than 12,000 people. 40 per cent of its visitors are tourists. The huge building is so well constructed that with its 8 acres of skylights, 70 per cent of natural light enters the mall. The mall is big enough to accommodate 25,000 school buses at any point of time, and has more than 500 stores covering 4.3 miles. If you spend just 10 minutes at every store, you will need more than three days to complete one visit!

129. The Pacific island of Guam does not have sand. The 'sand' found in the beaches is nothing but ground coral, and it is mixed with concrete for constructing roads!

130. Can you believe that the main library building of the Indiana University sinks over an inch every year due to the weight of its books?

131. Shopping malls in the city of Nottingham in England were the first to welcome visually challenged people by putting Braille signs to assist them.

132. The world's first undersea post office was in the Bahamas. This post office was initially a tube that stretched 200 feet below the surface of the sea, constructed by John Earnest Williamson's father. Williamson himself later converted this into a round chamber with a thick glass window and called it Williamson's Photosphere. He used the space to capture rare pictures of sea creatures in very high quality. Many of the stamps that were available in this undersea post office were images that had been captured from the Photosphere.

133. Many of the cinema halls in Greece do not have roofs. This is because the climate is quite warm for most of the year.

134. Do you know that Finland has around 1,88,000 lakes? No wonder it is called the 'land of the thousand lakes'!

135. Humboldt Redwoods, the third largest state park in California, has some of the largest virgin coast redwood trees in the world, some of them taller than a 30-storey building! The tallest tree measures nearly 117 m in height!

136. It is difficult to lose your way to the Victoria Falls in Zimbabwe. The waterfall is so loud that you can hear it 40 miles away!

137. The oldest roller coaster in the world was built in 1902. Located in Lakemont Park, Pennsylvania, they called it 'Leap-The-Dips'!

138. Lake Hillier in Western Australia is bright pink in colour. According to scientists, it is because of the algae present in the water.

139. In Australia, below a peak named 'Burning Mountain', near Wingen Village, there is an underground fire that has been active for 6000 years. The fire comes from a coal deposit below the sandstone. The initial settlers believed that the smoke had occurred due to volcanic activity!

140. Believe it or not, in Vientiane, Thailand, one can see red fireballs being shot up into the air through a river! No one knows why this happens, but according to a local myth, a

knows why this happens, but according to a local myth, a dragon or a snake called Naga passes through the area under the river water and puffs up fireballs into the air.

141. Imagine a busy highway passing through your office building. As weird as it sounds, such a building exists in Japan. The Gate Tower Building in Fukushima has two floors below the ground floor and 16 floors above the ground floor. The lifts don't stop through the fifth and seventh floors as these floors have been occupied by the highway!

142. A teahouse in China makes sure their customers deserve their tea before they get to the place! If you want to have tea at the Mt Huashan teahouse, gear up for an arduous journey consisting of many stairs, a tram ride, some dangerously placed planks aside the mountain, a long trek up a mountain slope and finally a walk along a spooky path!

143. Did you know that some parts of the earth do not receive sunlight for certain days? The little town of Viganella, on the Italian side of the Alps, did not receive any sunlight for about 84 days in a year due to the sun's position during winter, before 2006 (it would get blocked by a 1600-feet-tall mountain)! To solve this problem, the government installed a giant 26 x 16 feet mirror, controlled by a computer, on the side of the mountain to track the trajectory of the sun!

144. The post office in Arlington Heights, Chicago, allows customers to drive through the building and drop off letters and packages up to the size of a shoebox! Sounds like a cool postal service, doesn't it?

145. The largest underground city in the world is in Montreal. It covers a walkway of 32 km and accommodates around 2000 shops!

146. The Chapel of All Saints in Kutna Hora, Czech Republic, has a chandelier made of human bones.

147. Monaco and Vatican City are the smallest independent nations in the world. Each occupies less than 1 square mile. The other small nations include Nauru (South Pacific Ocean, 8 square miles), Tuvalu (Southwest Pacific, 10 square miles) and San Marino (Europe, 24 square miles).

148. Bolivia has the world's largest salt deposit. The Uyuni salt beds (Salar de Uyuni) reflect the entire sky when rainwater forms a thin layer on the top of this salt bed!

149. Can you believe that the world's largest single-dish telescope (305-metre-wide), in San Juan, Puerto Rico, attracts around 1 lakh tourists from all over the world ever year? The telescope enables scientists to study nearby planets and also the ionosphere.

150. How deep can you go to mine buried treasures? In South Africa, miners working in the Mponeng Mine (the deepest mine in the world) travel as deep as 2.4 miles underground to search for gold. To understand how deep this is, imagine 10 Empire State Buildings stacked on top of each other and placed underground!

151. Siberia has the largest forests in the world. The country has 25 per cent of the world's forested area.

152. The first restaurant in Hollywood opened in the year 1919 and was called Musso & Frank Grill.

153. America's very first subway system was built in Boston in 1897.

154. What is the most number of rooms you've seen in a house? The Buckingham Palace in London has around 600!

155. Las Vegas has the largest number of hotel rooms in the world, thanks to the number of tourists visiting this place from all over.

156. Do you want to experience a free fall from a 39-storey building? Then head to the Giant Drop in Australia, one of the tallest free fall rides in the world.

157. A city named Whitehorse, in Canada, has the cleanest air in the world.

158. Can you believe that there is a country with zero unemployment rate? The tiny country of Monaco is not only a tax haven, but also has the highest life expectancy in the entire world.

159. Lamprechtsofen-Vogelshacht, the deepest cave in the world, situated in Australia, has a depth of more than 5300 feet.

160. The Sutter Buttes is the smallest mountain range in the world. It is situated in California, outside Marysville.

161. There is a grove of pine trees with bent trunks in Poland, called the Crooked Forest. The trees were planted sometime around 1930. Nobody knows why they are so oddly shaped.

162. Have you heard about the Great Pacific Garbage Patch? It is a huge patch of garbage in the Pacific Ocean containing harmful chemicals and pollutants. The current size of the patch is more than that of the US!

Just Deserts

163. Deserts are uninhabited barren stretches of land. But have you ever wondered what percentage of the human population lives in deserts? Not less than 13 per cent!

164. How rarely can rainfall occur? Tidikelt, a town in the Sahara Desert, did not witness a single drop of rain for almost 10 years. And the Antarctic valleys near Ross Island have not witnessed rainfall for over 2 million years!

165. Can you believe that there are parts of Atacama Desert (situated in Northern Chile in South America) where it has never rained?

166. The University of Plymouth was the first university in the world to to offer a degree in surfing.

167. An event called 'doggy disco' is held in Italy where owners dance with their pet dogs.

168. Want to learn how to build an igloo? Canada has tour companies that provide two-day courses in igloo building.

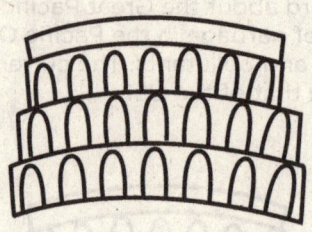

What in the World . . .

169. It is predicted that by the year 2025, China would have built 10 times more skyscrapers than those that stand in New-York-sized cities. But do you know that more than 60 million homes still remain unoccupied in the country and that some cities are completely empty even today? This is because China, just like Spain and Las Vegas, believes in building the entire city before inhabiting it!

170. California and Alaska may collide at some point of time. This is the conclusion of the NASA scientists.

171. The city of Mexico is sinking about 8 inches every year.

172. Three Mile Island in the United States is just about 2.5 miles long!

173. In Iceland, urban homes are not heated by a furnace or a water heater. Hot water or steam is piped into the cities from springs or natural geysers.

174. There are nearly 200 volcanoes in Japan. About 10 per cent of the world's active volcanoes are found in this country.

175. Do you know that the colour of the Great Pyramids was as white as snow once upon a time? It's because they were originally encased in white limestone, which faded over the years.

176. Are you planning a visit to Los Angeles? Think twice before you step out. It's the most polluted city in the US.

177. Some communities in the Canadian Arctic cover their windows in summer to keep the sunlight out while they sleep at night!

178. We all know that water expands when heated. But do you know that because of this phenomenon, the width of the Atlantic Ocean expands by almost 3 cm every year?

179. The Sears Tower in Chicago, Illinois, is made of 76,000 tons of steel!

180. Do you know that Argentia, in Canada, has almost 206 days of fog in a year?

181. SCROOGE, an organization in Charlottesville, Virginia, stands for Society to Curtail Ridiculous, Outrageous, and

Ostentatious Gift Exchanges. It was formed to keep the custom of gift exchanges simple and affordable during Christmas.

182. Do you want to participate in the oldest, longest and the biggest cross-country ski marathon in the world? Then pack your bags and head to Sweden to participate in Vasaloppet (translates to the 'Vasa' race), held on the first Sunday of March. 14,000 others will join you in the race!

183. Do you want to study different species of fish? Lake Malawi has the largest number of fish species in the world. Also known as Lake Nyasa, it is the third largest lake in Africa and is situated between Malawi, Mozambique and Tanzania.

184. Did you know that Canada and the US are the only two countries bordered by three oceans—the Atlantic, the Arctic and the Pacific?

185. The flags of all countries are rectangular, except that of Nepal.

186. Many countries have interesting signs or symbols on their flags. For example, the flag of Dominican Republic has a Bible on it, whereas the flags of Dominica, Egypt, Fiji, Kiribati, Mexico, Spain and Zambia have birds. The Cyprus flag has a map.

187. The full name of the Statue of Liberty is Liberty Enlightening the World.

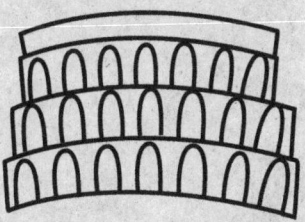

Cool Facts about Antarctica!

188

- Do you know of a continent that is still not owned by any other country and remains uninhabited by humans, reptiles and snakes? It is Antarctica.

- 90 per cent of the world's ice is present in this continent, out of which nearly 70 per cent is made of fresh water! If only we could tap this resource, it would solve the water shortage problem throughout the world.

- Ironically, Antartica is considered a desert as it is the driest place in the planet, with an annual precipitation of just 2 inches!

PLANT LIFE

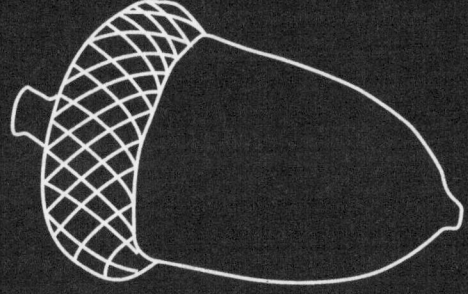

189

The Saguaro cactus is the largest cactus in the US and can survive for nearly 200 years if maintained under ideal conditions. It grows quite slowly and takes about 40 years to reach a height of 2.5 metres before it starts flowering. In fact, it starts developing its first branch only when it's more than 75 to 100 years old! Which means if you plant a Saguaro today, you may get to see your plant flowering, but chances are that only your children will be able to see the branches!

190. How do you calculate your age? By number of years? The age of the Saguaro cactus is calculated by its height!

191. According to archaeological studies, cannabis was the first plant to be cultivated by humans for garments, paper and linen.

192. How fast do you think a plant can grow? Bamboo plants can grow up to 36 inches in just a day!

193. Can you believe that plants respond to human emotions? Research indicates that plants that are pampered and stroked by their owners are healthier!

194. Do you know that many plant seeds can be coaxed to life even after centuries of dormancy if stored under ideal conditions?

195. The Welwitschia plant is so well adapted to survive even in dry conditions that it can live for a 1000 years.

196. Make a notch on a tree and observe as the tree grows further. If you have the patience to pursue this experiment for years, you will find that even if the tree grows, the distance of the notch from the ground remains the same!

197. How many varieties of red roses have you seen so far? There are over 900 types of red roses grown worldwide!

198. Ever heard of the word 'hydroponics'? It is a technique by which plants are grown only in water . . . without any soil.

199. The largest single flower in the world, the Rafflesia Arnoldii, which can be found in Indonesia, can stretch up to 3 feet of width and weighs close to 10 kg. The flower smells like a corpse in order to attract flies.

200. A mature oak tree draws 50 gallons of water every day!

201. We find blossoms of most trees in the branches. But in the case of the fig tree, the blossoms are inside the fruit!

202. The lifespan of an olive tree is not less than 1500 years. Syria first cultivated olives almost 5000 years ago.

203. Do you know that the maple tree has to reach 45 years of age and a diameter of 12 cm before its sap can be extracted?

204. Oak trees produce acorns only after they are 20–50 years old.

205. The African baobab tree has a circumference of close to 180 feet!

206. What makes the Mexican jumping beans jump the way they do? It's because of the moth larvae inside the beans.

207. If trees had a contest to keep their leaves for longer durations, they would be battling for the space closer to street lights. This is because trees that are not near street lights have been observed to shed more leaves!

208. Have you ever counted the number of rows in a ear of corn? There are 12–20, and if you consume one, you have eaten around 400–600 kernels!

ANIMAL KINGDOM

209

Do you know that a crocodile's stomach
can secrete so much acid that it can even
digest steel?

Nature of the Beast

210. Do you know that earthworms are herbivores and that they thrive on moist soil, eating roots and leaves? They can eat about one third of their body weight in just one day!

211. We have all seen bulls charging at red cloth. But do you know that bulls are colour-blind? They actually charge at the matador's waving cape, which can be of any colour—even blue or green!

212. Pigs are the only mammals that cannot look up at the sky.

213. Do you know that horses and rats cannot ever vomit?

214. We know that humans can get sunburnt. Do animals that mostly stay outdoors get sunburnt too? Yes, pigs do!

215. Kangaroos are the only four-legged mammals that cannot walk backwards.

216. Thank god we have sweat glands! Since pigs don't have them, they have to stay in water or mud most of the time to keep themselves cool.

217. Lion cubs cannot roar until they are at least two years old.

218. Tigers have striped skin, not just striped fur. Want to shave a tiger and confirm?

219. Do you know that leeches have 32 brains?

220. The cheetah, the fastest land animal, can pick up its speed to nearly 45 kmph from its static position within two seconds.

221. A single beaver is capable of cutting down 200–300 trees a year using its powerful front teeth!

222. Your teachers may think you're noisy, but we bet you can't be noisier than the male howler monkey, found predominantly in Central and South America. Can you believe that the noise made by this animal can be heard at a distance of 2–3 miles?

223. Gorillas are actually a type of ape and not a monkey. Then what distinguishes apes from monkeys? Monkeys have tails, apes don't!

224. Do you know the difference between horns and antlers? Antlers shed and grow year after year, but a horn never stops growing!

225. Did you know that mules have a male donkey and a female horse for parents?

226. Squirrels are quite absent-minded. Most of the time, they forget where they hide their nuts.

227. The oldest living animal to have ever been discovered was a 405-year-old clam named Ming. This shellfish was discovered in a seabed in the north of Iceland.

228. The duckbill platypus, a unique animal found in Australia, got its name because of its amazing snout, which looks like a duck's bill. The snout is soft and contains thousands of receptors that help the animal detect its prey. A platypus can store nearly 600 worms at a time in its cheek pouches!

229. Do animals have blue eyes? Only some black lemurs do!

230. There are nearly 1300 species of scorpions in this world, but out of these, only 25 of them are dangerous!

ANIMAL KINGDOM

231. Can you believe that a mole can dig a 300-feet-long tunnel in just one night?

232. Have you seen a turtle with three heads? Well, it's quite a rare phenomenon. A villager named Lin Chi-Fa in Southern Taiwan found this creature in his pond!

233. A crocodile cannot stick its tongue out.

234. 'Chameleon' is actually a Greek word meaning 'little lion'.

235. Chameleons and seahorses have eyes that can move independently, which means they can look in different directions at the same time and thus spot their predators easily!

236. The sleeping place of bats is called a 'roost'.

237. Different animals have different ways of escaping from their predators. The impala runs in a zigzag formation, jumping almost 3 metres high while doing so!

238. The horn of a rhinoceros is made of compacted hair.

239. A tiger's pee apparently smells like buttered popcorn. Are you inquisitive enough to try and smell it?

240. How do you blink? You close both your eyes at the same time, don't you? (Otherwise, it's called a wink, of course!) Hamsters and tortoises don't wink; they 'blink' with one eye at a time!

241. Alligators can lay about 40 eggs at one time, which hatch within 70 days.

242. Dentists have a potential patient in the alligator! After all, an alligator goes through 3000 teeth in its lifetime and has about 80 teeth at one time!

243. Bats are nocturnal in nature, which means they sleep during the day and are active during the night.

244. Do you know that a camel hump can weigh up to 35 kg?

245. The Arabian camel (dromedary camel) can gulp down around 100 litres of water in just about 10 minutes!

246
It's Raining Cat and Dog Facts!

- Do you know that dogs are descendants of the wolves that lived in the eastern parts of Asia 15,000 years ago?

- Dogs and cats can be left-handed or right-handed, just like humans.

- How many different sounds can you make? Dogs can make just about 10 while cats can make nearly 100 individual sounds.

- Human beings have nine muscles in their ears, whereas dogs have 17 and cats have 32! No wonder these animals are much more receptive to sound.

- Do you think only humans snore? Pet owners have reported that some cats and dogs snore too. Maybe they learnt it from their masters!

- Did you know that cats and dogs cannot sweat through their skin? Then how do they cool their bodies down? They lose water by panting and sweating through the pads of their feet, and nose!

- Living creatures have developed amazingly unique identities. Just like no two individuals have identical fingerprints, no two zebras have identical stripes and no two dogs have identical nose prints!

- Can you imagine a dog breed that can't bark? Well, the Basenji dog falls under this category. They are quite playful and active and express themselves through whines, screams and loud shrieks.

- What do you do when you are happy or pleased? Cats squeeze their eyes shut to express their happiness. The next time you see your pet shutting its eyes, wait for a few moments to see if he or she is really sleepy or just happy!

- Do you know that most cats don't have eyelashes?

247
Wild and Woolly

- Polar bears do not have coloured hair. In fact, their skin is black.

- Do you know that polar bears are left-handed?

- Polar bears have one predator—humans! Can you believe that polar bears are sensitive enough to smell humans who are 20 miles away?

- Polar bears can swim as far as 60 miles at once without any rest! Thanks to their habitation, their swimming skills have evolved marvellously.

- Polar bears have good appetites. Do you know that these animals can eat about 10 per cent of their body weight in just about an hour?

- Only female polar bears that are pregnant hibernate!

- Did you know polar cubs only start seeing or hearing a month after they are born?

248
In the Moo-d

- Do you know how cows sweat? Through their noses, because that's where they have their sweat glands. The next time you see a cow, observe its nose. You are most likely to find water droplets there.

- Cows, goats and sheep have teeth only in their lower jaws. The upper part consists of just one huge gum.

- Cows move their jaws at least 40,000 times in a day!

- A cow has not one, not two, but a total of four compartments in its stomach.

249
Irrelephant Facts

- The elephant is one of the three largest land animals in the world.

- Do you know that you can train an elephant to understand 60 different commands?

- Though elephants have knees, they are the only mammals who cannot jump. (Do you know which are the highest jumping mammals? They are the leopard and the puma; both can reach a height of 16.5 feet above land while jumping!)

- How much water do you drink in a day? You cannot possibly compete with an elephant: it drinks almost 80 gallons of water every day!

250
Bear in Mind

- Animals have their own way of marking territories. Male koalas have a dark scent in their middle chest, which they rub on trees to mark their territory.

- Koalas sleep close to 19 hours a day!

- The fingerprints of koala bears are so similar to that of humans that it could, in fact, create confusion in scenes of crime!

251
Slow, but Sure!

- Sloths can sleep for long hours, and hardly leave their tree for decades together.

- Sloths move so slowly that algae grow on their coats! Now you know where the expression 'lazy as a sloth' came from.

- Can you imagine eating and sleeping while hanging upside down? Well, sloths do that! In fact, the females give birth to babies hanging upside down!

- It takes about six days for a sloth to digest its own food.

252
Weighty Facts

- Do you know that hippopotamus milk is bright pink in colour? In fact, it's quite possible to mistake hippo milk for a glass of strawberry milkshake!

- How much grass do you think an adult hippo can feed on? 150 pounds in one night!

- Can you believe that a hippopotamus can survive underwater for up to five minutes?

- A hippo can easily live up to 40 years in the wild.

253
Rat Stats

- We know that a camel can stay for a long time without water. But do you know that giraffes and rats can survive longer than a camel without it?

- Rats can cause a lot of destruction in a very short period of time. Do you know that within 18 months, two rats can multiply to nearly 1 million?

- Why do scientists use rats for most clinical experiments concerning humans? It's got to do with our DNA. It matches more with a rat than a cat!

254
Prickly Facts

- There are around 30,000 quills on the body of an adult porcupine, and they are replaced every year!

- Do you know that the quills of a porcupine are soft when it is born? They harden a few hours after birth!

- Porcupines have a sponge-like filling in the quills that help them float on water so they can feast on water plants.

255
Slimy Facts

- How long can you sleep in one go? Desert snails can lock themselves inside their shells for about three years!

- A snail has thousands of teeth!

- Snails have their reproductive organs in their heads.

- Snails produce a slimy substance that protects them from getting hurt while moving on different kinds of surfaces.

256
Whither Do You Slither?

- There are no snakes and reptiles in Antarctica because of the extreme climatic conditions.

- Did you know that some snakes are born with two heads? And they often battle with each other for the same bit of food!

- Most snakes have not one, not two, but almost six rows of teeth!

- The black mamba, the largest venomous snake found in Africa, is also the fastest moving land snake. It can reach a speed of more than 12 miles an hour and can lift nearly 2/3rd of its body above the ground in order to get a full view of the surroundings.

257
Toad You So!

- It is hard for mice to survive in an area dominated by ornate horned frogs! These frogs have the ability to swallow an entire mouse, and are mostly found in Argentina.

- Frogs use their eyes to swallow food! They pull their eyes inwards towards their mouths and push the food down the throat.

- When a frog pukes, it throws up its entire stomach, cleans it and then swallows it back.

- Frogs never drink water! They only absorb it through their skin.

- The Spring Peeper (a frog species) can survive freezing winters even if nearly 65 per cent of its body water freezes into ice!

- Frozen wood frogs and frozen oysters continue living when thawed! In fact, wood frogs use the glucose present in their body to protect their vital organs in order to keep living during the frozen state!

258. Most living organisms have one heart, but earthworms have five!

259. The size of the largest earthworm recorded so far is 22 feet. It was found in South Africa.

260. Reptiles do not have oil glands, and they don't sweat.

261. Iguanas (herbivorous genus of lizards) can recognize people. They greet their human handlers differently, as compared to strangers.

A Little Birdie Told Us . . .

262. Birds can adapt to different environments and change their style of living accordingly. In fact, urban birds have been found to develop a fast singing style, as opposed to their melodious rural counterparts.

263. Birds do not sweat like humans and certain other warm-blooded mammals. This is because they do not have sweat glands. Many species just flutter their wings or lift up their feathers for air circulation or pant like dogs to keep their bodies cool.

264. Whooping cranes, the tallest birds in North America, have blue eyes when they are born. By the time they are six months old, their eyes become bright gold in colour. The female lays two eggs at a time and both the male and female sit on each of the eggs and incubate for about a month before the chicks hatch. Interestingly, the chicks know how to swim right after they are born, but take about three months to learn flying.

265. Have you ever seen any bird flying backwards? Only the hummingbird can! The hummingbird is the smallest bird in the world. It weighs less than a penny!

266. Eagles are not only powerful enough to kill deer, but they can even lift the animal and fly away with it!

267. An albatross can fall asleep when it's flying at about 25 miles per hour!

268. While gathering nesting material, the male and female scarlet tanagers communicate with each other by singing.

They primarily thrive in woodlands and have huge appetites. Can you believe that these birds eat more than 2000 gypsy moth caterpillars in less than an hour?

269. Unlike humans, pigeons are capable of seeing UV lights.

270. The Arctic tern is an amazing bird. During one migration cycle, it makes a trip from the Arctic to the Antarctic and back! Every migration cycle consists of a distance of nearly 20,000 miles.

271. Do you know that kiwis have nostrils at the tip of their beaks?

272. Ever heard of a 'barking bird'? Believe it or not, there is one—the Antpitta avis canis Ridgley.

273. Can you imagine eating with your head upside down? Flamingos can eat only this way!

274. Do you know that flamingos are actually white? They turn pink when they eat shrimps, which contain a red pigment. White flamingos are considered unhealthy or malnourished.

275. Owls have three eyelids.

276. Barn owls can hear so well that they are capable of hunting their prey even when it is totally dark.

277. Do you know how owls eat their prey? They can't bite or chew because they have no teeth, so they swallow their prey whole.

278. An ostrich's brain is smaller than its eye.

279. Penguins can survive extreme cold weather. But they are not found in the North Pole.

280. Mandarin ducks have whiskers, just like cats. Wondering what they do with their whiskers? They puff them out to attract females!

281
Fowl Play

- A hen lays up to 300 eggs every year. No wonder there are more chickens in the world than people!

- For producing just one egg, a hen has to be fed nearly four pounds of quality feed! The size of the eggs becomes larger when they grow older.

- The colour of the egg is linked to the colour of the earlobes! Chickens from brown eggs have red earlobes, whereas white-egg chickens have white earlobes!

- After laying an egg, the mother hen turns it 50 times every day! This is what prevents the yolk from sticking to the shell.

- Many people bite their fingernails when they are stressed. Chickens lose their feathers when they become stressed!

- How many living creatures can survive even after their head is cut off? One chicken survived for more than 18 months, headless! Incredible, don't you think?

- Can chickens fly? Scientifically, the answer is no. However, the longest 'flight' of a chicken recorded so far is 13 seconds.

282
Emus-ing Facts

- The emu is the largest bird in Australia. It can't fly, but it can run fast and swim quite well, unlike other birds.

- Do you know that emu eggs are large and green in colour? They are edible and also used for decorative purposes.

- Emus cannot walk backwards.

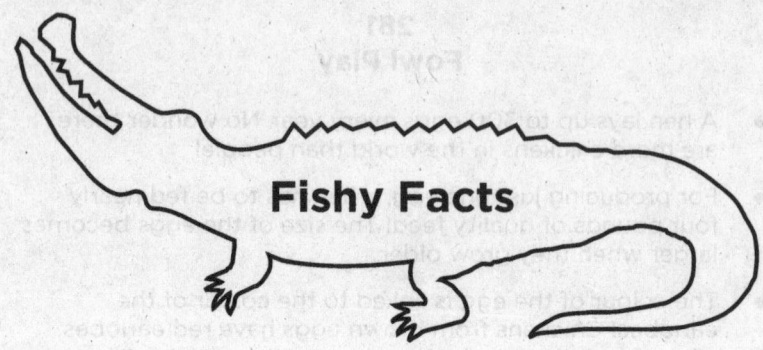

Fishy Facts

283. A well-trained freestyle swimmer can achieve a speed of about 4 miles per hour. Guess how fast fishes can swim. Some species have clocked a speed of 68 miles per hour!

284. The ocean sunfish can produce 30 million eggs at one go.

285. Bob Bateman of Canada once caught a salmon that had two mouths with two tongues and two sets of teeth.

286. Humans have 9000 taste buds on the tongue, whereas catfishes have nearly 27,000 taste buds! Wonder how flavoursome underwater food really is!

287. The velvet belly lanternshark has spines on its back that glow like lightsabres.

288. Did you know that candlefish, a type of ocean fish, are so oily that they were once burnt for fuel?

289. Garfish, a species found in the Eastern Atlantic waters, have unusual green-coloured bones. Though it's quite tasty, many people choose not to eat it because of its strange colour.

290. Do you know that there are 'amphibious fish' in the world? They can move around on land in search of another water source if their living habitat dries up. Species such as the snakehead fish can survive up to three days without a water source!

291. Imagine being born with eyes that fall off as they grow! The blind cavefish is the victim of such a condition. It loses its sight as it grows!

You're Squidding Me!

292. Scallops are known to have about a 100 eyes around the edge of their shells.

293. Have you heard of sea cucumbers? No, they are not a type of vegetable or fruit! They are actually marine animals that are cucumber-shaped. These animals, found mainly in the depths of the ocean, spill out their internal organs when they are threatened.

294. Seagulls can drink salt water without any problem. These birds have specially designed glands that can filter out the salt.

295. Lobsters need not worry about losing their eyes or claws. They usually grow new ones!

296. It is the male seahorse that gets impregnated, not the female. In fact, the males have pouches on their bellies and can hold up to 1500 babies at one time!

297. The giant squid, which can grow up to a length of 60 feet, does not have a backbone. It is also the animal with the largest eyes in the world!

298. Can you imagine a living creature without brains? Believe it or not, starfish and jellyfish don't have them!

299. A starfish is capable of turning its stomach inside out!

300. A starfish generally has five legs and an eye at the end of each leg!

301. Can you believe that jellyfish were in existence even before dinosaurs and sharks?

302. A hydra is perfectly capable of growing back its whole body even after it is cut in half. This marine animal thrives mostly in fresh water and is closely related to the jellyfish family.

303. What do you do when you feel nervous? Well, octopuses eat their own tentacles! Just like our nails, these tentacles grow back later!

304. How do you react when you are afraid? Octopuses that are originally brown in colour change to green or blue when they are scared.

Holy Mackerel!

305. According to a recent study, there are more venomous fish than snakes!

306. If you keep a goldfish in a dark room, it will eventually turn white.

307. Never feed dry fish food to your goldfish. This can constipate them.

308. How heavy can a blue whale be? Well, just its tongue weighs as much as an adult African elephant!

309. Can you believe that blue whales produce noise that can be heard nearly 800 km away?

310. Humpback whales can survive for about 95 years under ideal living conditions.

311. Do you know that humpback whales can communicate with each other in the ocean through their howls, moans and cries for hours together at a time?

312. Dolphins sleep keeping one eye open. And they can swim while sleeping!

313. Want to see pink dolphins? Head to the Amazon river!

314. Do you know that corals are actually marine animals and not plants as people commonly mistake them to be? Some species grow just about 1 cm a year!

315. The hard skeleton of the coral is nothing but calcium carbonate secreted by the individual polyps.

316. The Great Barrier Reef in Australia has grown to more than 2020 km, making it the largest coral reef in the world.

317. Do you know that oysters change their gender (male to female and vice versa) many times during their life?

318. In the Caribbean, there are some oyster species that can climb trees!

319. An oyster may take a few months or even a year to form a pearl. No wonder pearls are precious.

320
Deadly Data

- Do you know how sharks reproduce? While some of them give birth, others lay eggs. Whale shark eggs are the biggest in the world!

- Baby sharks 'escape' from their mothers as soon as they are born. The mothers see their own babies as their prey!

- Though sharks have lower and upper eyelids just like human beings, they cannot blink.

- The shortfin mako is considered to be the fastest shark species in the world. They can reach a speed of about 45 miles per hour and are incredible jumpers, reaching nearly 20 feet above water during their leaps.

- The orca whale (killer whale) belongs to the oceanic dolphin family.

- The orca whales are the largest of all dolphins.

- Orcas are known as the wolves of the sea as they hunt together in groups.

- How long can you hold your breath? An orca whale can hold it for nearly 15 minutes!

Flies, Fleas and Their Friends

321. Does music make you more productive? For termites, it does! It is believed that termites eat wood faster when listening to rock music. Do you know that there are 10 times more termites in this world than humans?

322. The Goliath Beetle is the biggest and the heaviest bug in the world. It can weigh up to 3.5 ounces.

323. Imagine living creatures eating themselves out of shortage or unavailability of food! Believe it or not, ribbon worms do. They can, in fact, survive even after eating nearly 95 per cent of their own body weight!

324. Can wasps get drunk? Of course, when they feed on fermented food!

325. Did you know that male cicadas are the loudest insects in the world? They are like crickets, and when they rub their abdomen, the sound can be heard as far as 1300 feet away!

326. A single mosquito has more than 40 teeth. Wonder how such a tiny creature has the space for so many teeth!

327. Do you know that only female mosquitoes bite humans? Male mosquitoes survive on natural resources.

328. Do you know that the common housefly can transmit some really deadly diseases?

329. The lifespan of a dragonfly is just a day.

330. Do you think humans can jump 1000 feet in the air easily? That is asking them to jump about 150 times their normal size. Well, a flea can easily achieve this feat. Never judge a creature by its size!

331. A firefly lives for about a week on an average. And it spends most of its life trying to find a mate.

332. Can you believe that the polyphemus moth, during the larva stage (first 56 days of its life), eats about 86,000 times its body weight?

333. The hawk moth caterpillar is quite a fascinating creature—it can inflate its thorax, because of which its head looks like a snake. That is how it protects itself when it senses danger.

334. A newborn emperor moth has a large tongue which shrinks as it grows. Finally, the moth dies of starvation as it is unable to eat.

335. Do you know that since its domestication, the silkworm moth has lost its ability to fly? You can get about 300 to 400 metres of silk on an average from a cocoon!

336. Can any creature survive after losing its head? A cockroach can remain alive for 10 days without its head, after which it starves to death!

337. A cockroach can hold its breath for about 40 minutes.

338. Cockroaches are so resistant to radiation that they may be the only creatures capable of surviving a nuclear war!

339. Cockroaches do not worry much if they break their legs! They grow a new one within a few days!

340. There are close to 2000 butterfly species found only in the South American rainforests.

341. Can you guess how many butterflies make an ounce? If you had monarch butterflies, it could well be around a 100 of them!

342. Living organisms generally smell with their nose. But butterflies are different . . . they smell and even taste with their feet!

343. Common species of garden caterpillars have nearly 250 muscles just in their head!

344. Can you believe that the silk produced by spiders is actually stronger than steel?

345. Spiders have claws at the edges of their legs.

346. Newborn spiders are generally nursed by their mothers. However, newborn crab spiders survive for several weeks only by eating their mother's limbs!

347. Imagine a spider species growing to a diameter of 50 cm! Unfortunately, the species, named Megarachne, is extinct now. It was found only as a fossil in Argentina.

348. Apparently, fried spiders taste like nuts!

349
Bees, Bees, Bees!

- Honeybees have been in existence for more than 20 million years now!
- A single colony of honeybees can consist of 30,000 to 50,000 bees in the summer.
- To make a pound of honey, about 10,000 bees visit nearly 2 million flowers and need to travel a distance of more than 55,000 miles. In just one trip, a honeybee visits 50 to 100 flowers and during its average lifespan of six weeks, it gathers about 1/10th of a teaspoon of honey!

- Each honeycomb cell has six sides. The nectar gathered by the bees consists of 70 per cent water. The bees remove excess moisture by fanning their wings on the open cells of the honeycomb. Finally, pure honey consists of just 17 per cent water!
- A single colony of bees can produce a 100 pounds of honey, which is what is harvested from the hive.
- Honeybees have five eyes out of which three are present on the top of their heads with light sensors. The other two have compound lens which give them their powerful vision!
- Do you know how honeybees communicate with each other? By dancing! When a bee finds pollen or nectar, it alerts other bees and with its unique dance movements, communicates the distance and direction.
- Do you know that male honeybees do not sting? They are called drones and they develop from unfertilized eggs. Their sole purpose is to mate with the queen bee!

350
Ant Attack!

- If you take an ant a few kilometres away from its anthill, it can still find the way back using its sense of smell.
- You cannot find ants in Antarctica, Greenland and Iceland. The climate does not suit them!
- How much weight can you lift? Well, ants can lift objects that weigh nearly 50 times their own body weight!
- Imagine 'hiring' ants to close your wounds. Sounds weird? But this was true for about 3000 years in South America, India and other parts of Asia. These ants were called 'carpenter ants'.
- The ant colony survives as long as the queen is alive. This is because after the queen ant dies, no new workers are born!
- For every surviving human in the world, there are close to a million ants!
- A person who studies ants is called a myrmecologist. Would you like to grow up and become one?

HISTORY

351

Way back in 1876, when the telephone was
invented by Alexander Graham Bell, only
six phones were sold!

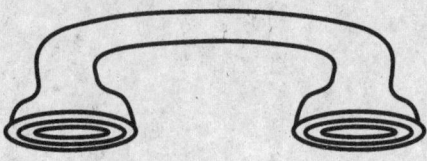

Kings And Queens

352. King George I was the ruler of England from 1714 to 1727, but he couldn't speak English! He was born and raised in Germany, so he never learned to speak the language. He ruled his country with the help of his ministers, thereby creating the first government cabinet.

353. Cleopatra married two of her own brothers. She got married to Ptolemy XIII when she was just 11 years of age. He died soon after the marriage and then Cleopatra married Ptolemy XIV, another younger brother, who died due to a disease.

354. Queen Elizabeth I owned 3000 gowns and always wore a necklace that had a perfume bottle attached wherever she went. And in order to hide the smallpox scars on her face, she would wear face paint.

355. The Ottoman Empire had seven emperors in succession in just seven months. While the first emperor died of burns, the second died of choking. The third emperor drowned and the fourth one was stabbed. The tragic end of their reigns continued as the fifth emperor died of heart failure and the sixth was poisoned. The last of these seven emperors was thrown down from a horse.

356. A Saudi prince grants the wishes of a 1000 people every month and is known for giving away thousands of dollars to the public.

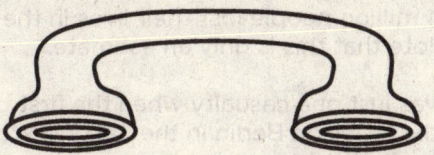

Bloody Battles!

357. Guess for how long the war between Zanzibar and England lasted. It happened in 1896. Zanzibar surrendered after 38 minutes! It's the shortest war in history.

358. 80 per cent of the males born in Russia in the 1923 did not survive the Second World War.

359. Imagine a battle being fought by naked men! Well, this was how General Joshua Milton Blahyi led his army into the battlefield during the Liberia Civil War. No wonder he was nicknamed General Butt Naked!

360. A bloodless war took place in 1839, between the Canadian province of New Brunswick and the US state of Maine. Although armed troupes were organized to fight, not a single gunshot was fired! The diplomats worked out a compromise.

361. Can wars last for more than a century? Well, the Hundred Years War actually lasted for 116 years, between 1337 and 1453. It was a series of wars between the royal houses of England and France. The conflict was so prolonged that the war was divided into three phases—the Edwardian War (1337 to 1360), the Caroline War (1369 to 1389) and the Lancastrian War (1415 to 1453). Finally, France emerged victorious.

362. The United Nations (UN) was established in 1945 post the First World War, to promote international cooperation and global peace. But isn't it shocking that even after the UN was established, there have been nearly 140 wars?

HISTORY

363. Over 54 million people lost their lives in the Second World War. Note that this is only an estimate.

364. There was just one casualty when the first bomb was dropped by the Allies on Berlin in the Second World War—an elephant in the Berlin Zoo.

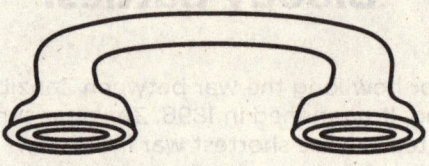

Settling Scores . . .

365. A simple coin toss settled a dispute for naming a city in 1844, when the city of Portland in Oregon had to be named. Heads went for Portland and tails for Boston.

366. The two largest cities in Australia are Melbourne and Sydney. In 1908, following the rivalry between these two cities contesting to be the capital of Australia, a common location was chosen, about 248 km from Sydney and 483 km from Melbourne. This gave rise to Canberra, the current capital of Australia. Unlike the other Australian cities, Canberra is an entirely planned city.

367. Alaska initially belonged to Russia. Can you believe that the US just had to pay 2 cents an acre to buy the region?

368. In 1819, Spain had a $5 million debt with the US. Guess how the country cancelled this debt? Florida was sold to the US at this price!

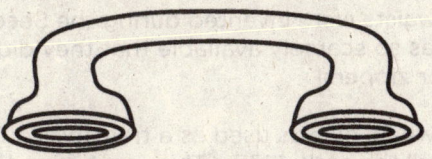

Insane Inventions

369. Toilet paper was used only by emperors in 1391. These 'priceless papers' were produced in China at that time.

370. Do you know that the Volkswagen Beetle was known as the 'people's car'? It was the brainchild of Adolf Hitler, who wanted to introduce an affordable car in the market, which could be used by an average German household for transporting two adults and three children (an average family size during those times). In fact, this still remains the most manufactured economy car in Germany.

371. Lawrence Richard Walters (also called Larry Walters), an American truck driver, manufactured a home-made flying machine by tying 45 weather balloons filled with helium to an ordinary patio chair! He rose to a height of 15,000 feet.

372. Who were the first passengers of the first hot-air balloon flight manufactured by the Montgolfier brothers Joseph and Jacques? Well, no human flew in this case. A rooster, a duck and a sheep were placed in a basket and suspended below the hot-air balloon. A crowd of more than 1,30,000 spectators along with Louis XVI, Marie Antoinette and the French court watched in awe as the balloon flew for eight minutes and covered a distance of 2 miles in Versailles before it brought back the occupants safely to the ground!

373. Toothpaste was initially packaged in metallic tubes. Due to shortage of metal post the Second World War, plastic tubes were used and the practice has continued since then.

374. The modern toothbrush that we use today originated in China. The bristles were initially made of hogs' hair or the manes of horses and mounted on ivory handles.

HISTORY

375. Elastic waists were invented during the Second World War. Metal was so scarcely available that they did not want to use it even for zippers!

376. Sperm whale oil was used as a transmission additive for some cars until the early 1970s. This was banned after the Endangered Species Act of 1972 was enforced.

377. Tablecloths were once used as towels! People used to wipe their hands on the cloth after eating.

378. How did people manage to keep the air cool when air conditioners had not been invented? They covered their furniture with white cotton slipcovers.

379. During the 1800s, butter churners and washing machines were propelled by dogs that walked on treadmills to generate power for running them.

380. Most women use lipstick to colour their lips today. But do you know that during the Louis XIV era, lemons were used for this purpose?

381. Did you know that the Whamo-O product Hula-Hoop, invented in 1958, has been in existence for almost 3000 years now? Just that, at that time, the hoops was made of grapevine!

382. Did you know that people with hearing difficulties used ear trumpets before the hearing aid was invented?

383. Imagine remaining still for eight hours for a snap! Well, that was how much time the first camera took to capture a photo!

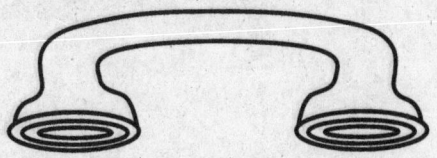

In Ancient Egypt . . .

384. Do you know that people in ancient Egypt did not approve of facial hair? They considered it as neglect of personal hygiene!

385. In ancient times, for Egyptians, the death of a pet was more than just a personal loss for the owners.

386. How much importance did Egyptians give to their pet cats? Well, when cats died, they were buried with their masters or in special cemeteries created just for them.

387. We know people buy jewellery as gifts for family and friends, but did you know that ancient Egyptians would buy trinkets for their pet crocodiles?

388. Did you know that Egyptians slept on pillows made of stone?

389. Ancient Egyptians kissed each other not on the cheeks or forehead, but on the nose!

390. Egyptian pyramid builders were known to include lot of garlic in their diet. They believed that it would increase their body strength.

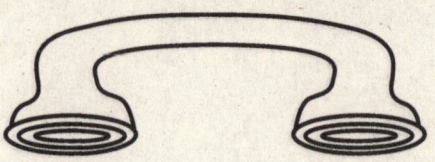

When in Rome . . .

391. What do you think could be common between flamingo tongues, parrotfish livers and pheasant brains? They were all considered delicacies by Roman emperors!

392. How did people take baths when there was no soap? Well, we know that Romans used to clean themselves with olive oil and scrape off dirt from their bodies with a type of blade called strigil.

393. Do you know that walnuts were used by Romans to cure ailments of the head? It's apparently because the nuts were shaped like human brains!

394. Did you know that prickly porcupine quills were used by early Romans as toothpicks?

395. What is the most unusual ingredient that can go into a toothpaste? Ancient Romans used human urine as an ingredient!

396. Can lemon be an antidote for poisons? Well, that's what Romans in the 3rd century believed.

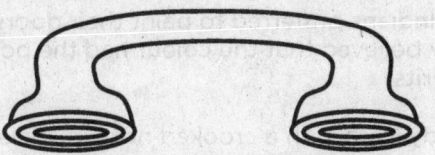

Ways of the World

397. During the 1900s, Spain enjoyed an overwhelming harvest of grapes. The government wanted to entice the citizens to consume the fruit before it rotted. So they spread the notion that if people consumed this fruit on New Year's Day, it would foretell their future depending on the taste of the fruit. Till today, people in Portugal, Spain, Peru and Mexico eat 12 grapes at the stroke of midnight on New Year's Eve. It is believed that the taste of each fruit predicts their future for each month. Different types of fruits are popular in different countries. For example, while the Turks favour pomegranates and believe that the fruit brings them fortune, the Chinese feast on oranges and tangerines.

398. Do you know that children from wealthy families in ancient Greece were dipped in olive oil at birth? This has nothing to do with any tradition, but was done to keep them hairless during their lifetime!

399. During the reign of Peter the Great, Russian men who grew a beard had to pay a special tax!

400. In the 1900s, women had to be unmarried and between 17 and 26 years of age to be a telephone operator!

401. Have you heard of a wedding ceremony where sandals are exchanged by the couples? This is weird but true in the case of the ancient Incas of Peru. The couples took off their sandals and handed them to one another and this declared them officially married!

402. Did you know that peacocks and swans were cooked and served during special Christmas dinners in the Middle Ages?

HISTORY

403. Native Indians preferred to paint their doors blue. This is because they believed that the colour had the power to keep away bad spirits.

404. Anybody born with a crooked nose in ancient Rome was expected to become a leader in future.

405. Long ago, many people thought that eating tomatoes would help you fall in love. Hence, they nicknamed these fruits 'love apples'!

406. In the 19th century, Japanese women actually dyed their teeth black. They believed that it would keep their teeth healthy!

407. People in medieval Europe would mix gold powder in water and have it as a drink to relieve pain in the limbs.

408. In ancient Egypt, women used to wear wax perfume cones. The wax would melt due to their body heat and let out a nice fragrance! Innovative, huh?

409. Ever thought that skulls could be used as currency? As spooky as it sounds, it was done in Borneo once upon a time!

410. Romans used to make toothpaste by crushing mouse brains. They believed it would keep their breath fresh and their teeth pearly white!

411. Germans believed that a cow's lick could cure baldness!

412. Doctors in ancient Egypt used the jolts from electric catfish to relieve arthritic pain.

413. People in Martha's Vineyard, near Massachusetts, were bilingual between 1692 and 1910. One of the languages they spoke was English and the other was a sign language with a special dialect! Post 1692, the number of deaf people in the region gradually increased because of some genetic hearing problem. Hence, in order to communicate with the deaf population that grew considerably large over the years, everyone had to learn sign language!

414. Before the 1800s, shoes were not designed separately for left and right feet!

415. It is said that China developed silk and kept it a secret for close to 2000 years!

416. Do you know that the Christian calendar was created by the Ukrainian monk Dionysius Exiguus?

417. Would you believe that even during the 1980s, there was a country which did not have telephones? If you were in Bhutan during this time, you would have been aware of this fact!

418. As late as the 1930s, most Siberian people, especially the nomads, preferred teabags over metallic coins as currency! This was because apart from using it as currency, tea could be consumed as food in times of hunger. It was also brewed as medicine for cold and cough.

419. Did you know that some of the Bangkok police were once asked to wear 'Hello Kitty' armbands as punishment? Unfortunately, this plan backfired when most of the policemen happily took these armbands home, considering them souvenirs!

420. Can anyone build earthquake-proof walls? The Incas, known for their fine stone masonry, did manage to create them. They built walls with stones that fit in to each other so precisely that the stones would only slightly move and resettle during an earthquake, but never collapse! They used a building technique that was a combination of suppression of resonant amplification and energy dissipation!

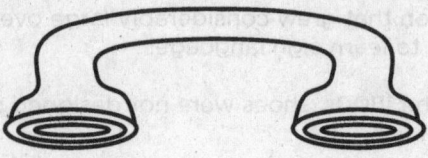

Peculiar Professions

421. During the early years of the Industrial Revolution, alarm clocks were neither reliable nor affordable. How do you think people managed then to get up on time? Well, they hired other people to wake them up and paid them a few pence every week! This was actually a popular profession in Ireland and England at that time. These people were called 'Knocker-ups'! The knocker-ups would use a heavy stick to knock on the door of their clients every morning. For houses situated on higher floors, they used lightweight bamboo sticks which were high enough to reach the windows. Even police constables used to take up this profession to earn additional income during their morning patrols!

422. We have seen clowns in circuses, but have you heard of clowns performing at funerals? Funeral clowns were popular in ancient Rome. These clowns had to dress up like the person who was dead and mime his style, gestures and expressions! It was the responsibility of the funeral clown to make the grieved relatives laugh. Funeral clowns who performed at any emperor's funeral were paid heftily, sometimes even more than the gladiators!

423. During the 15th and 16th centuries, many English courts kept a 'whipping boy'. The king was mostly never around to personally discipline his child and the tutors at the court found it quite difficult to enforce discipline. Since they were not allowed to punish the prince directly, they hired a whipping boy. A whipping boy was assigned to a particular prince and every time the prince misbehaved, the whipping boy was punished instead of the prince.

424. Have you heard of professional applauders? They are hired to clap after a performance. Such people are called 'claqueurs', originating from the French word 'claque', meaning clap. This was quite common during classical times, especially in French opera houses and theatres, before it spread to other parts of the world.

425. Between the 16th and 19th centuries, dogs were the favourite pets of almost every European household. It was quite common for them to accompany their owners even to church services. At that time, the church appointed dog whippers to manage these pets. These officials were given the authority to even remove them from the church if the animals were disruptive or unruly. In some villages, a portion of the land was dedicated for this purpose. In fact, the 'Dog Acre' park in Birchington-on-Sea was actually used by the dog whippers in the past! Later, these officials were hired to manage even the stray dogs in the village.

426. Can you specialize in laughter? Yes, you can! You need to study gelotology, and you would be called a 'gelotologist'.

427. Can you imagine being in a profession that requires you to study different types of faeces? The study of faeces is called scatology, and the people who study it are called scatologists.

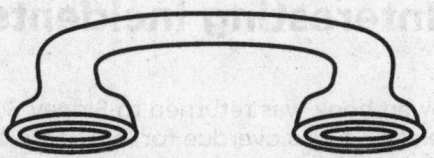

Keeping You Posted . . .

428. Do you know that Great Britain was the first country to issue postage stamps, in the 1840s?

429. The Columbian state of Bolivar has the smallest stamp in the world. It was introduced in 1863 and measured just 9.5 x 8 mm!

430. The advertising industry targeted the back of 3-cent US stamps for advertising various products as early as 1883.

431. Did you know that the first self-adhesive stamps were issued on 10 February 1964?

432. In 1973, Bhutan issued a musical record stamp. It played the national anthem of the country when placed on a record player!

433. Can you believe that way back in 1963, the postage rate for letters was determined by how much light would pass through the letter? The lesser light that went through, the costlier the rate of postage!

434. Ever seen a banana-shaped stamp? Well, this was once issued by the Pacific island of Tonga and it was in circulation from 1969 to 1985!

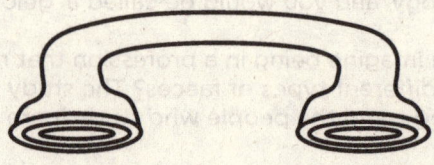

Interesting Incidents

435. A borrowed book was returned to Sidney Sussex College in Cambridge after it was overdue for 288 years! Wonder what the person who took the trouble to return it had to pay as penalty.

436. Have you seen a river flowing backwards? This happened to parts of the Mississippi river during an earthquake on 16 December 1811.

437. Westminster, London, experienced total darkness in 1890 for a whole month! There was no sunrise in December that year.

438. Did you know that the Eiffel Tower, the brainchild of Gustave Eiffel, was meant to be dismantled in 1909, after its twenty-year permit was over? It was retained as it played a highly important role during wartime communication.

439. Can you believe that the Niagara Falls on the American side was actually stopped for several months in the year 1969 as the engineers considered restructuring it? However, the plan was later dropped due to huge expenses.

440. Have you ever heard of 'Waterloo teeth'? They were dentures that were sold for many years throughout Europe after the tragic Battle of Waterloo. These dentures were made from actual human teeth extracted from the corpses of soldiers in the battlefield. Most of these teeth belonged to healthy, young boys who fought in the battle.

441. In the year 1948, the Universal Declaration of Human Rights was written by the United Nations. This document has been translated into about 321 languages and dialects, which make it the most translated document worldwide!

442. We all know about the devastating First World War, which killed around 14 million people. But do you know that more people were killed during a flu epidemic that followed this period? This epidemic cost 20 million lives.

443. In London, during the summer of 1958, the Members of the Parliament were forced to leave the House of Commons chamber due to a bad sewage smell from the river Thames.

444. In 1848, the Niagara Falls actually stopped flowing for twenty hours due to ice blocking the Niagara river. What a huge ice block that would have been!

445. In 1926, a waiter in Budapest left a suicide note in the form of a crossword. In fact, the police took help from the public to solve it!

446. Do you know that Tycho Brahe, the renowned 16th-century astronomer, is not only famous for his mathematical computations but also for his nose replacement? Due to differences over a mathematical formula with Manderup Parsberg, his third cousin, he entered a duel to resolve the differences during which he lost a part of his nose! He then had to get a replacement nose made of a combination of silver and gold and attach it using glue!

447. In 1976, when doctors went on strike in Los Angeles, the death rate actually dropped by 18 per cent!

448. What happened in the November of 2001 in Singapore that you ought to know about? For the first time ever, there was a 'World Summit on Toilets'! Started by the World Toilet Organization, an international NGO for improving sanitation and toilet facilities worldwide, the summit is held every year in various cities around the world. Do you know that the summit was held in New Delhi, India, in the year 2007? The founding day of this summit was declared as the World Toilet Day!

449. The Krakatoa volcano eruption that occurred in Indonesia in the year 1883 caused a huge impact all over the world. The eruption was heard thousands of miles away. The colour of the sunset was reported to have changed because of the massive dust that emerged from the explosion.

450. Can you believe that over 6,00,000 people succumbed to the deadly Spanish influenza epidemic in 1918?

451. Did you know that the American Automobile Association was formed in 1905 to warn motorists of police speed traps?

452. The first telephone book, which was published in 1878 in New Haven, Connecticut, was just a page long and had only 50 names in it!

453. A molasses flood occurred in Boston in January 1919, killing 21 people and leaving 150 injured.

454. Can one be hired just to flush toilets? Well, this actually happened in 1989 at Gator Bowl, Jacksonville, Florida, during the Christmas weekend, before the annual New Year's college football game. The 23-member crew had to keep flushing the toilets to avert freezing of the pipes! In 1983, freezing and damage of water pipes cost up to $4,00,000!

455. The first ever speeding ticket was handed out in 1895 by the Hampshire police when a man 'crossed the speed limit' of more than 6 miles per hour!

456. Can you imagine sneezing continuously for two and a half years? Believe it or not, that was the fate of a 12-year-old girl in England who started sneezing in January 1981, not expecting to record the longest sneezing fit in history!

ART
AND
CULTURE

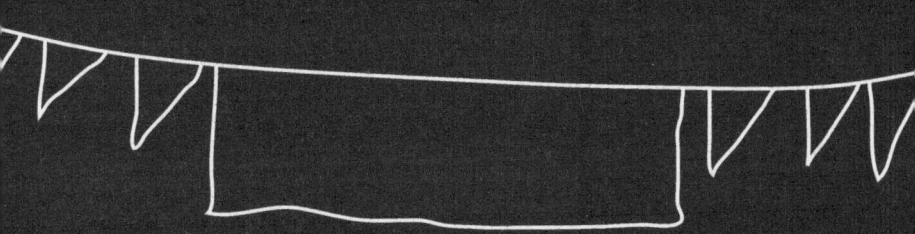

457

The colour green is a symbol of freshness, vibrancy, rejuvenation and survival. For many people around the world, it signifies prosperity and abundance. In fact, people around the world eat green, leafy vegetables as part of New Year celebrations. Cabbage, kale and chard are the most popular choices of green leafy vegetables that are cooked or consumed in their raw form. For example, Germans consume sauerkraut (finely shredded sour cabbage), whereas people in Denmark cook sweetened kale flavoured with cinnamon.

458. The interpretation of gestures varies between countries. If you shake your head from side to side in India, you are saying 'no'. However, in Sri Lanka, it is interpreted as 'yes'!

459. Do you know why brides carry bouquets of flowers? In olden times, it was to hide body odour!

460. An Amish man grows a beard (without a moustache) once he is married. He is never without a beard after that.

461. In Korea and a few other countries in East Asia, people calculate their age not from physical birth but from conception!

462. The whole of the US celebrates Halloween on 31 October while just one place—Carson City in Nevada—celebrates Halloween a day before. This is because 31 October is celebrated as Nevada Day.

463. Have you heard of 'Squirrel Day'? It is celebrated in Illinois in the town of Olney, to honour the 200 albino squirrels surviving in the town. In fact, as part of the celebrations, a priest blesses the squirrels, wishing them long and healthy lives! What a wonderful idea to promote respect for other living species!

464. We have often seen sculptures of warriors on horseback in parks and public places. But do you know that the way the horse is depicted in these statues has a strong significance? If the front legs of the horse are in the air, it means its rider has died in battle. If just one front leg is lifted in the air, the person was wounded in a battle because of which he met his end. If all four legs are placed on the ground, the person died of natural causes.

465. The Uape Indians, living in the Amazon, have a weird way of remembering their relatives. They mix the ashes of the recently cremated person with alcohol and all the family members of the deceased drink this concoction!

466. Lent, the 40-day preparation season before Easter, is a period of repentance and fasting in reflection of the suffering of Jesus Christ. In Ivrea, Italy, a colourful carnival called 'Battle of Oranges' is held during the three-day pre-Lenten period. The participants are supposed to throw oranges at each other! The celebrations have been in existence for centuries though until the 19th century, beans were used by the combatants.

467. Barbie Dolls do not show their teeth while smiling in Japan. Their lips are closed and the skin colour is lighter. This is because in Japan, women close their mouths even when they laugh, as part of their etiquette.

468. Be careful when you gift flowers to a Russian! Do you know that, on romantic occasions, Russians gift flowers only in odd numbers while for funerals, they bring flowers in even numbers?

469. If you love watermelon and you also like cheese, wonder how the combination would work? Ask the people of Israel or Egypt. It is a tradition to eat watermelon with feta cheese in these parts of the world.

470. Do you know the real name of Santa Claus? The tradition was inspired by a bishop in Myra town named Saint Nicholas, who was known to be kind to children.

471. Did you know why flags are flown at half-mast following a death? One of the many beliefs is that this gap above the flag is for the 'flag of death' as it reminds people of the impact, power and existence of death.

472. Residents of High Wycombe, UK, have a tradition of weighing their mayors before and after their term. This practice began way back in 1678 as people wanted to know whether the officials were corrupt and getting fat with public money!

473. Do you know why men in Japan are commemorated as they reach the age of 60? It is to recognize that they no longer have to bear the responsibilities of a mature adult!

ART AND CULTURE

474. The Japanese consider four to be an unlucky number. Wonder why? Well, the Japanese word for four sounds quite similar to the word for death.

New Year's Day

475

- In many countries around the world, lobsters and birds are considered unlucky to be eaten on New Year's Day. However, people feast on pork dishes as pigs are believed to be symbols of progress and abundance. While some countries like Hungary, Spain and Cuba consume roast pork, sausages are more popular in Germany.

- Lentils are edible pulses that look like tiny coins and expand while cooking. Hence, they are believed to signify prosperity and are popularly consumed during New Year. Italians and Germans eat sausages with lentils.

- The Japanese prepare toshikoshi ('year-bridging'), an interesting dish of buckwheat noodles in soup on New Year's day. People slurp the noodles and do not bite them while eating because they believe that if the noodles break, it will bring them bad luck!

- While people in Poland follow the tradition of consuming pickled herring on New Year's Day, boiled cod is popularly eaten in Denmark. Baccalà (cod fish that is salted and dried) is consumed by Italians whereas the Japanese include shrimp and fish eggs (herring roe) as part of the New Year menu. Germans eat carp and not only that, they carry fish scales in their pockets for good luck!

- Can the shape of a dessert be significant? Round or circular foods are believed to signify proper completion of a year. That is the reason why doughnuts are popular among the Hungarians and the Dutch, whereas in Holland

and Italy, fried dough balls sweetened with honey and sugar are eaten on New Year's Eve. In fact, according to Dutch folklore, if one's stomach is filled with these special pastries, it is immune to sword attacks from nasty beings. In Holland, people stuff raisins and fruits in these dough balls and call them 'ollie bollen'. The Greeks and the Mexicans bake ring-shaped cakes and hide goodies like small trinkets and coins in them, thus adding an element of surprise to their favourite dessert!

Merry Christmas!

476

- The Orthodox Christmas Day celebrates the birth of Jesus Christ on 7 January. Before the Gregorian Calendar system (that is currently followed) came into existence, where the date was revised to 25 December, Christmas was celebrated on 7 January according to the Julian Calendar. Hence, it is also called the Old Christmas day!

- Do you know the names of Santa's reindeers? They are Donner, Prancer, Dancer, Dasher, Cupid, Comet, Blitzen and Vixen.

- 'Jingle Bells', the famous Christmas song by James Pierpont, was initially written for a Thanksgiving programme. At that time, it was called 'The One-Horse Open Sleigh'.

- Do you know that the earliest Christmas tree was actually a pyramid made of wood and was decorated with evergreen boughs and apples?

- As part of their Christmas celebrations, people in Czech Republic make little boats out of empty walnut shells, place burning candles in them and float them in a bowl filled with water. They believe that if the shell makes its way across the bowl, it is a sign of good health and long life. However, if it sinks during its journey, it brings bad luck.

Ludicrous Laws from Around the World

US Laws

477. Do you know that US Census information (that is collected every 10 years) is open to public inspection only after 72 years by law?

478. A federal law in the US, implemented in the year 1969, states that it is illegal for US citizens to have any contact with extraterrestrial beings or their vehicles!

479. Bingo games can't last more than five hours in North Carolina.

480. Quitman, situated in Georgia, enforced a law that prevented chickens from crossing the road.

481. In Alabama, it is illegal to wear a fake moustache that may provoke laughter in church. We wonder if they can grow a real moustache that looks funny!

482. Shaking carpets in a street is illegal in Cambridge, Massachusetts.

483. There was a law in Bellingham, Washington, in the olden days, according to which it was illegal for a woman to take more than three steps backward while dancing!

484. You need to be a registered blood donor to participate in duelling in Uruguay.

485. A patient is not allowed to pull a dentist's tooth in Yukon, Oklahoma. Wonder how many patients are really interested in doing that!

486. You are allowed to sell 'only locally made ice cubes' in El Paso, Texas.

487. Cutting a cactus is illegal in Arizona.

488. In Denver, Colorado, you cannot share your vacuum cleaner with your neighbour!

489. Can a state enact a law to enforce bathing? Well, in Kentucky every citizen needs to take a bath at least once every year.

490. You think only humans can be punished by law? Not true. An elephant was tried and hanged for murder in 1916 in Erwin, Tennessee!

491. Did you know that hunting whales on a Sunday is illegal in Ohio?

492. You need to have a hunting licence to catch mice in Cleveland, Ohio.

493. There is a law in Idaho that does not permit gifting a candy box heavier than 50 pounds.

British Laws

494. In the UK, you are not allowed to hang a bed out of your window!

495. In the UK, you cannot paste a stamp with the British monarch depicted on it upside down.

496. If a dead whale is found on the British coast, the head of the whale is legally owned by the king, whereas the tail goes to the queen! In addition, she may use the bones for her corsets.

497. In England, the Speaker of the Parliament is not allowed to speak!

498. Can you imagine the weirdest penalty that can be given for committing suicide? It is death! Yes, that was the law in England during the 19th century.

499. Beating a carpet or a doormat in the street after 8 a.m. is considered an offence in London!

500. In London, it's illegal for a cab to carry corpses or rabid dogs.

501. It is forbidden to die in the Houses of Parliament in London.

502. Royal Navy ships entering the Port of London need to treat the constable of the Tower of London to a barrel of rum.

503. Residential Internet connections should not be faster than 56 K in Uxbridge, England.

Canadian Laws

504. According to Canadian law, it is illegal to board a plane when it is in flight. (Is that even possible?)

505. You are not allowed to purchase an item worth 50 cents by paying only in pennies in Canada.

506. In Gananoque and Oshawa, people have to compulsorily clear off the snow on the municipal sidewalks near their homes. If it is not done within 24 hours after snowfall, the municipal authorities clean the sidewalk but the home owner would be charged for the same in the next tax bill. Nice way to delegate social responsibility!

507. In Nova Scotia, you are not allowed to water the lawn when it is raining.

508. Business signs in Quebec have to be in French. If somebody wishes to provide an English translation, the sign in French should be written in a font twice the size of the English one.

509. A law enforced in Cobourg town in the Ontario province in Canada, states that your water trough in the front yard needs to be filled before 5 a.m. in the morning!

European Laws

510. Can you marry a dead person? You can in France! It is called a 'posthumous marriage' and is predominantly done for emotional reasons, to get over the death of the beloved or to legitimize children.

511. In France, you cannot name a pig Napoleon.

512. Do you know that it is forbidden by law to sell ET dolls in France? The law states that it is illegal to sell dolls with faces that do not resemble humans!

513. It is a rule that every Belgian child should compulsorily take harmonica lessons at the primary school level.

514. Never feed pigeons in Italy, unless you want to pay a fine of a few hundred dollars. This law was introduced to protect the local buildings from pollution caused by pigeon poop!

515. It is forbidden to wash your car, dry your clothes or mow your lawn on a Sunday in Switzerland! Also, you are not allowed to flush your toilet after 10 p.m.!

516. You are supposed to own a licence before you purchase television sets and VCRs if you are living in Norway.

517. In Finland, speeding tickets are based on how much money a person makes. Once, a 27-year-old had to shell out 1,16,000 pounds as he was the heir of a sausage empire!

518. In Denmark, every time you purchase a plastic or glass bottle, you will be charged a fee, which will be reimbursed when you return the bottle to any of the supermarkets. A wonderful measure to reduce, recycle and reuse, isn't it?

519. An interesting Danish law states that a person eating at an inn cannot be charged until he feels he is full. Also, water cannot be charged unless served with a lemon slice or ice.

520. In Germany, offices, however small they are, need to have a view of the sky.

521. Can pillows act as weapons? Apparently, they can. Germans consider pillows to be 'passive weapons'.

522. In Germany, an official approval is required before infants are named!

Rest of the World

523. Chewing gum is not sold in Singapore. People are fined for spitting in public places, feeding birds and polluting the environment or dirtying public toilets. No wonder Singapore is one of the most pristine places in the world.

524. People who want to remain fit but have irregular exercise routines should join one of the traditional Japanese companies. Even today, they conduct exercise sessions for workers in the morning in order to prepare them for work during the day.

525. Weathermen in Moscow can be penalized for inaccurate forecasting.

526. In Sudan, men are not allowed to wear make-up!

527. In China, people driving power-driven vehicles are not allowed to stop at pedestrian crossings! They are given a warning or even charged with a penalty!

528. In Australia, you need to be a licensed electrician to change a light bulb in your own home!

529. You are not allowed to use water guns during New Year celebrations in Cambodia. No mention about real guns though!

530. The Thailand currency (Baht) has a picture of the king. If you happen to step on it even by accident, you may have to serve a jail term or suffer a serious beating.

531. The Philippine government has adopted an innovative method of regulating traffic. The citizens are forbidden to take their cars out one day in a week, depending on their licence plates. This rule is enforced from 7 a.m. on the forbidden days. Cars that have licence plates ending with the numbers 1 or 2 cannot be taken to the road on Monday. The rule similarly holds for numbers 3 and 4 on Tuesday, 5 and 6 on Wednesday, 7 and 8 on Thursday and 9 and 0 on Friday. The rule is relaxed during weekends.

532. Some Shanghai hospitals insist that nurses wear lipstick while on duty.

All about Art

533. Leonardo da Vinci was known to be an animal rights activist. In fact, he used to buy caged birds only so he could free them.

534. The Renaissance period flourished in Rome. But ironically, none of the Renaissance artists, sculptors or musicians were born in this city. They were all brought to Rome for specific projects during the 15th and 16th centuries and they departed once their work was over!

535. Have you ever seen paintings made of cow dung? The French artist Michel Vienkot used it while creating his pictures!

536. Dwight Kalb, a Chicago artist, sculpted a statue of Madonna using just ham. He needed 180 pounds of it!

537. Did you know that Vincent Van Gogh sold only one of his paintings in his entire lifetime? The coveted painting is called *The Red Vineyard*.

538. Can you believe that about 15,000 years ago, cavemen added talc as an ingredient to paint?

539. Native Americans used blood for painting due to the permanent nature of its stain.

540
The Mona Lisa

- Do you know that the famous *Mona Lisa* painting showed three different versions when viewed under X-ray?
- Leonardo da Vinci took 10 long years just to paint Mona Lisa's lips!
- The actual name of the portrait is La Giaconda.
- Da Vinci's inspiration behind the portrait was the wife of Francesco del Giacondo, a middle-class merchant of the Renaissance period.
- *The Mona Lisa* has no eyebrows. It was considered fashionable in Renaissance Florence to shave off your eyebrows.
- Da Vinci did not date or even sign his most famous painting!
- Tadahiko Ogawa, a Japanese artist, recreated the famous *Mona Lisa* painting from burnt toast bits.

Picture This!

541. The longest running scripted show in television history is *The Simpsons*. Set in Springfield, a fictional town, this satirical parody of the American middle-class lifestyle has managed to entertain television viewers for over two decades.

542. In 1963, the movie *Cleopatra* was made with a budget of $44 million. It would cost $300 million now!

543. Can you believe that a 17-minute battle scene in a movie cost $40 million to produce? We're talking about one of the scenes in the blockbuster movie *Matrix Reloaded*.

544. The next time you watch any of the *Godfather* movies, observe that whenever an orange is shown on screen, a death or a close encounter is about to happen!

545. Do you know how soap operas got their name? In the early days of American TV, daytime dramas were originally used to advertise soap powder. In fact, the advertisers would weave a story around the usage of their soap products!

546. Did you know that the extras in the movie *Braveheart* were actual reserves from the Irish Army?

547. During the shooting of *Fight Club*, Brad Pitt chipped his tooth by accident. The chipped-tooth look suited his character, so he continued filming without getting it fixed. He got his tooth capped only after the shooting of the movie was completed.

548. Martial arts superstar Bruce Lee's moves were too fast to be captured on regular film. So technicians had to slow the film down in order to show his moves clearly.

549. Did you know that Michael Jackson owned the rights of the South Carolina State anthem?

550. Sylvester Stallone initially earned a meagre $1.12 for a small day job where he had to wrap smelly fish and take out poop from lion cages!

551. Jim Carey worked as a part-time janitor and a security guard at the age of 15, after his father became unemployed. Carey credits this tough phase in his life for his love of comedy as he used to visit several local comedy clubs after a hard day's work to get rid of stress!

552. The Oscars given during the Second World War were made of wood because metal was scarce at the time.

553. Guess who was named 'Man of the Year' in 1982 by *Time* magazine? For the first time, a machine received this honour. It was the computer!

554. Greer Garson delivered the longest Oscar speech in history after receiving the Best Actress award for the movie *Mrs Miniver* in 1942. Her speech was more than five minutes! That was a great honour considering that the granted time limit for the acceptance speech is just about 45 seconds!

555. Quincy Jones has received no less than 77 Grammy Award nominations in his lifetime. What a star, huh?

556. Talent knows no age. Henry Fonda won the Oscar for Best Actor at the age of 76, making him the oldest actor to win the award!

557. As of 2012, Meryl Streep has received 17 Oscar nominations and 26 Golden Globe nominations. Out of these, she has so far won three Oscars and eight Golden Globe awards.

558. Guess who we're talking about. This legend became a cartoonist after he was rejected by the army for being underage! If he had gone on to become a soldier, he would've probably never become the Walt Disney we know of and love.

559. Do you know that Walt Disney, the man who created the iconic Mickey Mouse, was afraid of mice?

560. Disney's *Tangled* is the most expensive animated movie to be ever made. The estimated cost was around $260 million. It also happens to be the second most expensive movie of all time!

561. Charlie Chaplin made 81 films in his 50-year career!

562. Even today, many Indian families believe in the traditional arranged marriage system. In fact, Ken, Barbie's boyfriend, was not sold in India until a few years back as it clashed with this institution.

563. In 1998, the killer whale Keiko, the main attraction of the Disney movie *Free Willy,* was shipped from Mexico City to Newport, Oregon by United Parcel Service.

564. Did you know that the popular Donald Duck comic series was banned in Finland because the comic character did not wear pants?

565. The Disney film *Mulan* is based on a 1500-year-old Chinese story.

566. How much would you pay for a pair of slippers? Can you believe that the ruby red slippers used in the movie *The Wizard of Oz* were bought in an auction for a hefty amount of $6,60,000?

567. For every second of a cartoon animation, the cartoonists have to create 24 individual drawings!

568. Did you know that Bulova Watch Company was the first to have a TV commercial, on 1 July 1941? For the 10-second-long announcement and a place in history, they paid a price of $9!

569. Have you observed that watch/clock advertisements mostly show the time as 10:10? The reasons are many, but the most widely accepted one is that the watches look symmetrical and the details of the watch/clock are clearly visible when the hands are positioned like that.

570. Real milk is not used in milk ads. In most cases, it's white paint mixed with a thinner.

571
The Mickey Mouse Club

- Mickey Mouse's image is the most reproduced in the world. It is found in more than 7500 items worldwide!

- By 1933, Mickey Mouse had received 8,00,000 fan letters.

- Interestingly, Mickey Mouse was banned in Romania in 1935. The authorities thought that a huge 10-foot rodent would terrify children. How did they permit Dracula?

- Observe the number of fingers Mickey Mouse has. Only four!

- What is the Italian name for Mickey Mouse? Topolino.

Pottermania

- Nearly 16,000 children from the US and the UK auditioned for the role of Harry Potter. The boy who finally bagged the role, Daniel Radcliffe, hardly had any acting experience!

- Can you guess how many times the make-up artists had to apply the lightning-bolt-shaped scar to Harry Potter and his body doubles? Not less than 5800 times throughout the series, out of which the original actor Daniel Radcliffe had to be re-scarred about 2000 times!

- J.K. Rowling doesn't really have a middle name. Anticipating that young boys might not want to pick up a book written by a woman, her publishers insisted on using just her initials on the books. So the K in J.K. Rowling stands for her grandmother's name, Kathleen.

ART AND CULTURE

FOOD AND DRINK

573

How do you figure if your egg is fully cooked?
Just spin it! If it easily rotates, it is cooked.
If it wobbles, it's still raw!

Facts to Chew On

574. Saffron is the most expensive spice in the world.

575. Can you really make delicious dishes with bugs? David George Gordon has listed 33 recipes in *The Eat a Bug Cookbook*, published in 1998.

576. Do beetles taste like apples? Well, people who have tasted them say so!

577. Roasted termites is a delicacy in South Africa.

578. Did you know that the largest seed in the world is that of the coconut?

579. Want to get rid of onion breath? Chew parsley after you eat onions!

580. Chicha, a traditional drink made in Latin America, contains human saliva for added taste!

581. Have you seen the word 'carrageenan' in commercial ice cream packs? It's a seaweed extract added to the ice cream to keep it crystal free.

582. A flavouring extract named castoreum is added to a lot of baked dishes. This extract is made from the anal glands of beavers! The next time you find the label 'natural flavouring' in the ingredients list for vanilla, strawberry and raspberry, think twice!

583. How can proper use of land resolve the issue of food shortage? Dedicating just 1 acre of land to high-quality wheat can produce enough bread to feed a family of four for 10 years!

584. Did you know that the tiny, humble pea is the oldest known vegetable?

585. From where do onions get their distinctive smell? It's the sulphur that they soak up from the soil. In order to avoid shedding tears while chopping onions, refrigerate them before cutting. Do you know that chewing gum while cutting onions can save a few tears?

586. One of the first vegetables to be canned for commercial purposes was carrots! Do you think carrots are always orange in colour? There are purple, white, yellow and red varieties too!

587. Contrary to popular belief, wild rabbits do not eat carrots!

588. Have a sweet tooth but on a diet? Grab a beetroot today. It's the vegetable with the most amount of sugar!

589. Do you know that the peanut is actually not a nut? It's a legume.

590. Have you heard of sauerkraut? It is nothing but finely shredded fermented cabbage with a sour taste, rich in vitamin C. It is believed that Captain James Cook always took sauerkraut during his voyages to prevent scurvy that occurs due to the deficiency of vitamin C.

591. Are you diet conscious? Increase the consumption of radish in your diet. Ten whole radishes contain just 8 calories!

592. Do you have tooth problems? Include lots of milk and cheese in your diet then, because they are believed to fight tooth decay!

593. If you overcook eggs, you will see a green ring around the yolk. Do you know why? A chemical reaction occurs between sulphur that is found in the white part of the egg and the iron found in the yolk!

594. Have you ever wondered why milk is white? It contains a protein called casein, which is white in colour.

595. To make just one pound of peanut butter, you need more than 700 peanuts!

596. There is a simple way to remove chewing gum from hair or clothes. Just apply peanut butter on the area!

597. French fries are the most ordered single food item in American restaurants. In fact, about 1/3 of the potatoes produced in the world are sold as French fries.

598. Do you know why chicken wings are sometimes called 'buffalo wings'? It's because the dish originated in Buffalo, New York.

599. Do you know why pizza restaurants fill their interiors with an abundance of red, yellow or orange colours? These colours are supposed to stimulate hunger!

600. During the 1830s, ketchup was sold as a patented medicine under the name 'Dr Miles' Compound Extract of Tomato'.

601. Can you believe that since Heinz started making ketchup in 1876, it has not changed its recipe?

602. Can you believe that there are around 175 sesame seeds in every McDonald's Big Mac bun?

603. There are around 600 different pasta shapes!

604. Did you know that the first American pasta factory was opened by Antine Zerega in Brooklyn, New York, in 1848?

605. Sandwiches have been in existence for over 250 years. The first sandwich was made in the year 1762. The name comes from the Earl of Sandwich, John Montagu, as he was the first person to request for meat between pieces of bread.

606. Salted hot potatoes were served as a dessert in a napkin during the 18th century.

Facts, Sweet and Sour

607. Want to avoid the rush of caffeine in the morning to charge you up? Substitute your cup of coffee with an apple. In fact, it will increase your efficiency and also get rid of your morning blues!

608. The science of cultivating fruit is called 'pomology'.

609. Ever heard of 'Persian apples'? They are nothing but peaches! There is an interesting story behind how these fruits got this name. Iran was called Persia before 1935. Peaches were cultivated in Xian, China, for nearly 3000 years before they spread to Persia (now Iran) and Russia when Chinese traders dropped the pits along the trade routes. Later, Europeans assumed they came from Persia. Alexander the Great carried these fruits from Persia to Greece. And that's why they came to be known as 'Persian apples'.

610. Do you know that lemons contain more natural sugar than strawberries? In fact, 70 per cent of a lemon is made up of sugar. The sour taste comes from the 30 per cent of citric acid present in the fruit. Strawberries contain 60 per cent starch and only 40 per cent sugar! Now we know that even tastes can be deceptive!

611. Many fruits ripen even after being plucked from a tree, but not an orange!

612. Do you know that the cucumber is actually a fruit and not a vegetable?

613. Pineapples are also called 'ananas'. It is a Caribbean word which means 'excellent fruit'.

614. More than 90 per cent of watermelon content is just water. But do you know that these fruits are native to the Kalahari Desert of Africa?

FOOD AND DRINK

99

615. How do you know if a full watermelon is ripe? Knock on the outside using your fingers. If it is ripe, it will sound hollow.

616
Go Bananas!

- Interestingly, it was Alexander the Great who discovered bananas in India when he invaded the nation in 327 BCE.

- How many different types of bananas do you think there are? Not less than 500!

- Iceland produces bananas in an ingenious manner. The soil there is heated by geysers, making it possible to cultivate these fruits.

- Have you heard of 'red bananas'? Unlike most other varieties, which have yellow-shaded peels, the peel of a red banana is maroon in colour initially, and becomes dark purple when it turns ripe. They are rarely eaten fresh and are more popularly consumed in the form of baked desserts.

- Want to enjoy a low-fat ice cream? Then try this simple recipe—freeze a banana and put it through a food processor or blender. It's as yummy as ice cream!

- Do you know that banana trees are actually giant herbs and not trees?

- Did you know that banana leaves were used for treatment of serious burns by people in the Pacific Islands?

We All Scream for Ice Cream!

617. Did you know that ice cream originated in China?

618. Ronald Reagan has declared July as National Ice Cream Month in the US.

619. Baskin Robbins once developed a ketchup-flavoured ice cream, but discontinued the flavour when it didn't do well. No surprises there!

620. Some parts of the UAE are known to have ice creams that are made from camel milk!

621
Sweet Treats

- Chocolate was initially a drink enjoyed only by the elite as only the rich and the affluent could afford it.

- The first chocolate house was opened in England in 1657. At that time, a pound of chocolate cost 13 shillings.

- Chocolates can kill dogs as some of the constituents directly affect the nervous system and the heart.

- Can you imagine how Kit Kat would taste without one of its key ingredients? During the Second World War, there was a shortage of milk, so Kit Kat was made without it!

- There is a popular candy bar in the US called The Three Musketeers, because it contains three different flavours—vanilla, chocolate and strawberry—in the same package. Manufactured by Mars, it was introduced in the year 1932. Restrictions during war and rising costs of sugar forced the company to phase out strawberry and vanilla at a later point of time. This popular chocolate bar celebrated its 75th anniversary in the year 2007.

622
Pop . . . Goes the Corn!

- Do you know that the word 'popcorn' is derived from the word 'poppe', which means 'explosive sound'? How apt!

- How did popcorn become such a popular snack for cinemagoers? It dates back to the Second World War when there was a sugar shortage because of which candies weren't available. As a result, theatre owners cashed in on popcorn.

- Here's a simple tip to store popcorn for a long time. Just store the popcorn in a moisture-free container and freeze it! It will remain fresh and crunchy for at least three weeks!

Beverages

623. Buttermilk can be a refreshing drink on a hot, tiring day. The name is misleading though, because it does not contain any butter! It comes from the fact that buttermilk is the liquid that is left after churning butter from fresh cream or milk.

624. People in the western regions of China, Tibetans and Mongolians drink tea mixed with salt!

625. Do you know that the oldest known recipe in the world is for beer?

626. Tender coconut water is not just a refreshing drink. It has incredible healing powers too. Do you know that doctors in some countries would inject tender coconut water into humans to save their lives?

627. For every can of Pepsi that you drink, remember that you are also gulping down seven teaspoons of sugar along with it!

628. Honey is the safest thing to consume as even the most harmful bacteria cannot survive in it for a long period.

629. Wines taste better when they are grown in poor quality soil. Surprising, isn't it? This is because the plants have to 'work' harder for the yield.

630
Wake up and Smell the Coffee!

- 1,3,7-trimethylzantihine—Ever heard of this chemical name? Many of us are commonly addicted to this substance, especially in the mornings. It is nothing but caffeine.

- In one year, a coffee plant grows beans just enough to produce 1.5 pounds of coffee every year?

- Before coffee was brewed, coffee beans were chewed for nearly four centuries!

- Coffee contains thousands of chemicals in traces. About 26 constituents were tested on rats and they caused cancer!

- Do you think decaffeinated coffee is 100 per cent free of caffeine? Nope, about 2 per cent of caffeine still remains!

- Did you know that acorns were used as a coffee substitute during the American Civil War as coffee was scarcely available in the South?

FOOD AND DRINK

THE
HUMAN
BODY

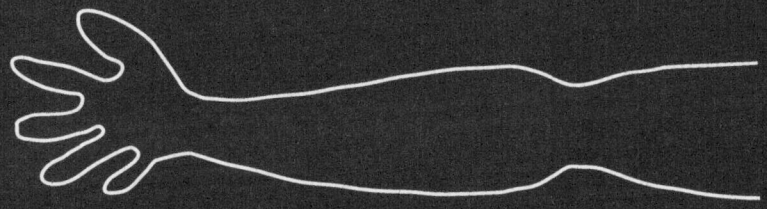

631

The human body is made up of some weird, awesome proportions. For example, your thumb measures the same as your nose. Your foot and forearm are the same length.

The Five Senses

632. Human beings have five powerful senses—sight/vision, smell, taste, hearing and touch. Do you know which among these five senses requires more brain power? It is vision!

633. The human eye can detect nearly 10 million individual colours. In fact, it can detect 500 different shades of the colour grey, which itself is a variant of black!

634. Do you know that the pupil of your eye responds to things based on your emotions? It expands when you see something pleasing. Similarly, it dilates when you are looking at someone you love or hate!

635. Have you heard of the term 'glabella'? It refers to the space between your eyes. Do you know that this space is almost equal to the size of your eye?

636. Just try this once. Rub your eyes gently and open them. Do you see some colourful spots or stars in front of you? These are called 'phosphenes'.

637. Do you know that we shed our eyebrow hair every three or five months?

638. There are nearly 5 million scent receptors in our nose. A human nose can distinctly detect and remember as much as 50,000 different scents. But the way each nostril registers smell varies! While the left nostril can accurately detect the smell, the right nostril makes it more pleasant! Have you wondered why you have a runny nose when you cry? The tears from your eyes drain into the nose and come out of it!

639. 'Bless you!' is what you hear when you sneeze. This is because you are almost reborn every time you sneeze! Your heart stops for a millisecond when you sneeze. And some of your brain cells die! Can you sneeze with your eyes open? Never! How powerful can a sneeze be? Well, if you sneeze too hard, you may even fracture a rib! On the other hand, if you try to suppress it, you can even die as you may end up rupturing a blood vessel in your head or neck. Do you know that apart from dust, allergy and foreign particles entering the nose, some people sneeze when they are exposed to light (natural sunlight or torchlight shined into their eye)?

640. Try this. Plug your nose and close your mouth. Can you hum now?

641. Do you know that 85 per cent of the population can roll their tongue into a tube?

642. It is common for human beings to think in the language they use the most. In what language do you think people who are born completely deaf and have learnt sign language think in? In sign language, of course! They can see themselves using signs in their minds like we hear ourselves talking in our minds! This is because deafness changes the way the brain works and deaf people have to be taught sign language to ensure that they develop their inner voice.

643. The tongue is the strongest muscle in the human body. Just as every person has a unique fingerprint, every individual has a unique tongue print too.

644. Do you know our taste buds also have a lifespan? We acquire a new taste bud every 10 days!

645. The next time you chew food, note which side of your mouth you use. Interestingly, most right-handed people use the right side of the mouth to chew, while left-handers use the left side!

646. Do you know that we can taste food only because it is mixed with saliva?

647. Which is the hardest substance of the human body? It is the tooth enamel, the mineralized surface of the tooth!

648. The chemical in toothpaste that helps fight cavities is called stannous fluoride.

649. How long do you think a yawn lasts? Six seconds, approximately!

650. Dieting reduces the secretion of saliva, which leads to a dry mouth and causes bad breath! You don't want to suffer from this by starving yourself, do you?

651. Here's an important tip for personal hygiene! Dentists advise that toothbrushes should be kept at least 6 feet away from the toilet area to avoid any bacteria from the flush.

652. Guess which is the most common non-contagious disease that people all over the world suffer from? Tooth decay!

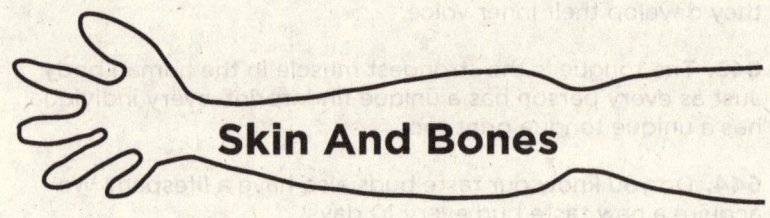

Skin And Bones

653. Do you know that 6 pounds of your body weight comes only from your skin?

654. Do you think only snakes shed their skin? We humans do it too! We shed skin in the form of flakes. On an average, a person sheds nearly 40 pounds of skin during his or her lifetime!

655. People with dark skin do not develop wrinkles as fast as people with light skin.

656. Mark a square inch in any part of your body. It will have 1,90,00,000 skin cells!

657. Did you know that our skin is home to more than 500 different species of bacteria? If you were to put all the bacteria in a human body together, you would get 10 times more bacteria than human cells! Most number of bacteria in the mouth is found on the surface of the tongue. More than 400 species are found only in the colon!

658. Even though we shed our skin, tattoos don't vanish. The dye is injected to the lower layer of the skin, which is called the dermis. The layer we shed is called the epidermis.

659. If you develop swelling from an insect bite, just apply a few drops of lemon juice on the affected area. The swelling will subside in a few hours!

660. Do not scratch a mosquito bite. To soothe the itching, just cut open a clove of garlic and rub it on the affected area.

661. Do you sweat profusely or have bad body odour? Then you have live bacteria in your skin that is multiplying, dying and decomposing rapidly.

662. The human body contains trillions of blood cells. Do you know that millions of blood cells die every second and are replaced by an equal number?

663. The most common blood group is Type O while Type AB is the rarest.

664. There are about 45 billion fat cells in an average adult.

665. Human beings are born with nearly 300 individual bones in the body. Once the person become an adult, many of the smaller bones join together to make single bones and the overall count reduces to just 206.

666. The stapes bone, located in the middle ear, is the smallest bone in the human body. The largest bone is the thigh bone (called femur), which is stronger than concrete and capable of lifting nearly 30 times its own weight!

667. Which is the hardest bone in the human body? It is the jawbone.

668. Did you know that the human skull is made of eight interlocked bones that form the head and 14 bones in the facial region? The only movable part of the skull is the lower jaw.

669. There are 54 bones in your hands, including the ones in your wrists!

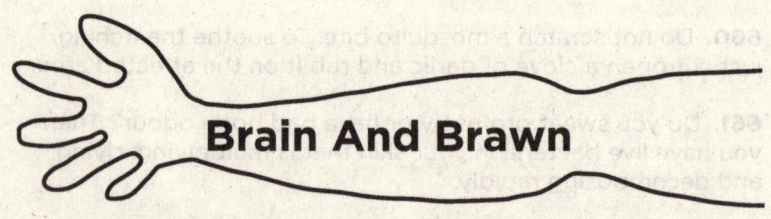

Brain And Brawn

670. Your fingernails grow about four times faster than your toenails! Also, if you are right-handed, the nails on your right hand grow faster and vice versa. Among the fingernails, the nail on the middle finger grows the fastest while the nail on the thumb grows the slowest.

671. Fingernails grow faster in cold weather.

672. Do you know that human toenails contain gold? It will take nearly 2 billion toenails to extract just 1 gram of gold though!

673. Once you swallow your food, it takes about seven seconds for it to reach the stomach!

674. The acids that are produced during digestion can, in fact, digest your stomach itself. Your stomach produces a new mucus layer every second week in order to protect itself from getting digested!

675. Which is the largest internal organ of the human body? It is the small intestine!

676. An adult can hold up to 1.5 litres of material in his or her stomach!

677. The palms of your hands and the soles of your feet are the only two places in your body which do not tan or grow hair. Out of the 2 million sweat glands present in our body, a majority of them are found in these two parts.

678. Do you know which of your five fingers is the most sensitive? It is your index finger.

679. Do you know that most people suffer insect bites on their foot than any other part of the body? Now you know where to apply the most amount of mosquito repellent.

680. Every time you take a step forward, you use 200 muscles!

681. Do you know that a person can manage to survive a few weeks without food but a person who lacks sleep is likely to die sooner?

682. Learning more than one language makes you smarter!

683. You should be wary if you have high fever. If the temperature goes above 107.6, it may end up causing brain damage!

684. It is not possible to tickle yourself. Your brain knows that you are about to tickle yourself and hence ignores the sensation.

685. People who are more than 35 years old start losing about 7000 brain cells every day which are never replaced!

686. What do the following have in common—a banana, a fruit fly, a mouse, a cow and you? Not much, except that you share around 50 per cent of your genetic design with the banana, close to 60 per cent with the fruit fly, near to 75 per cent with the mouse and almost 80 per cent with the cow!

687. One in 20 people are born with an extra rib in their body. Most of them are, of course, not even aware of it.

688. Do you know that your body has invisible stripes? Human cells arrange themselves in a striped pattern, but are mostly invisible as their colour is the same as the skin. Some people with certain medical conditions can actually see these stripes if their cell colour is different from their skin tone. These stripes are called Blaschko's lines. They were named after the dermatologist who discovered it—Alfred Blaschko.

689. People on crash diets lose hair faster. You don't want to become bald while trying to become thin, do you?

690. How many calories do you need to burn to lose just a pound of fat? A whopping 3500 calories!

691. Can you name some organs in the human body that do not stop growing? They are your ears and your nose. But do you know which parts grow the fastest? The bone marrow, hair and skin! Among these, the hair is the fastest growing tissue.

692. Most people think that the liver is an organ. It is actually a type of gland.

693. Do you know that the right lung is larger than the left so it can accommodate the heart?

694. The heart, one of the most vital organs of the human body, hardly weighs a pound.

695. Do you know that your right lung takes in more air than the left lung?

696. A pint of your blood could actually save four other lives!

697. Can you believe that nearly 400 gallons of recycled blood are pumped through our kidneys in just one day?

698. It will take less than a 1000 mosquitoes to suck all the blood out of your body in a single day.

699. Which is the largest artery in the human body? It is the aorta, whose diameter measures almost equal to that of a garden hose. It originates from the left ventricle and delivers oxygenated blood to other parts of the body by circulation.

700. The tonsils are two balls of tissues present in the left and right sides of your throat. They form an efficient infection fighting system in your body that prevents foreign substances from being swallowed or breathed in. Sometimes, this defence system can cause problems when it is infected by virus or bacteria, which can lead to discomfort and sore throat. In some severe cases, they have to be removed.

701. One of the weirdest cases of abnormal tooth growth happened in 1977, when a 13-year-old boy named Doug Pritchard had a tooth growing out of his left foot!

702. Ursula Kuschfeldt, a woman from Berlin, had nearly 3110 gallstones removed from her gall bladder!

703. Hans N. Langseth (1846–1927) of Norway had a 17.5-feet-long beard. Nobody has managed to break this record yet!

704. How frequently do you cut your fingernails? Shridhar Chillal holds the record for growing the longest fingernails on the left hand (measuring more than 20 feet!). After growing his nails for nearly 60 years, their weight has become so immense that Chillal suffers nerve damage, permanent deafness in his left ear and also disfiguration of his fingers.

Lee Redmond, a lady from Salt Lake City, used to hold the Guinness World Record for growing the longest fingernails on both her hands! The nails measured an average of 35 inches in length at the end of 30 years of their growth! However, she lost them in 2009 following an accident.

705. Zeng Jinlian of China was the tallest woman who ever lived, with an unbelievable height of 8 feet 2 inches! She died when she was just 17 years old. She could not stand straight as she had a severely deformed spine.

706
Left and Right!

- Most people use their left hand more while typing.

- The possibility of twins being left-handed is quite high.

- Try writing with both your hands at the same time. Leonardo Da Vinci could write with one hand and draw with the other!

- James Garfield, the 20th President of US could write in two languages (Greek and Latin) at the same time, using both his hands!

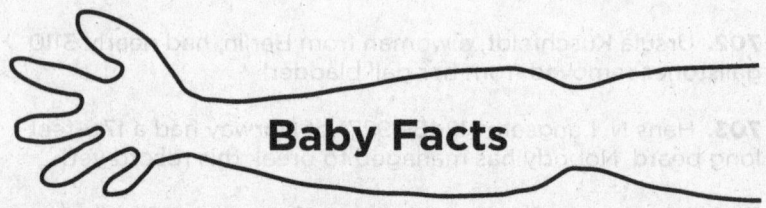

Baby Facts

707. Did you know that a human embryo, when just four weeks old in the mother's womb, is smaller than a grain of rice?

708. Babies are so sensitive inside the mother's womb that they can hear sounds at lower frequencies that are normally inaudible to human beings!

709. A foetus can also get hiccups.

710. We know that fingerprints are unique to every individual. But do you know when you first get these? When you are still an eight-week-old foetus!

711. A foetus can yawn when it's only 11 weeks old!

712. Do you know babies cannot distinguish colours when they are born?

713. Try breathing and swallowing at the same time. Well, this is an ability you lose as you grow up! Infants can breathe and swallow food at the same time.

714. Though infants cry quite often, they do not produce tears for the first three months!

715. Do you know that infants do not have kneecaps when they are born? These develop between the ages of two and six only.

716. Do you know that infants dream more than adults? Does it mean that they are more creative?

717. Is it possible for babies to be born with teeth? It only happens to one in 2000 babies.

718. It is believed that babies who are exposed to dogs and cats during the first year of their life have fewer chances of developing allergies later.

719. Want to measure the intelligence of a person? Check the zinc and copper levels in their hair! Intelligent people have more amounts of these minerals.

THE HUMAN BODY

Fear Factor

720. Can anybody fear fun? The answer is yes—cherophobia is the word that denotes fear of fun!

721. The fear of marshmallows is called althaiophobia.

722. The fear of vegetables is called lachanophobia. People who suffer from this condition start sweating and become completely panic-stricken if they see certain vegetables on their plate.

723. Did you know it's possible to be not just phobic, but even allergic to water? Mainly due to the chemicals present in water, some people develop a rare allergy known as aquagenicpruritis. Doctors can help, but due to its rarity and the causes being uncertain, treatment can be dubious!

724. Ever heard of people suffering from a fear of ducks watching them? Such a phobia exists and it's called anatidaephobia! They suffer from the apprehension that there is a duck watching them from some part of the world!

725. There are people who have nightmares about going bald. They're called peladophics.

726. Can people fear clowns? Believe it or not, some do and this is referred to as coulrophobia!

727. Do people have a fear of teeth? Yup. It's called odontophobia.

728. Do people have a fear of telephones? Yes. Predictably, it's called telephonophobia!

729. Can you imagine people having an intense fear of cooking? It is called mageirocophobia.

730. If you suffer from paraskevidekatriaphobia, friggatriskaidekaphobia or triskaidekaphobia, it means you have a fear of the number 13.

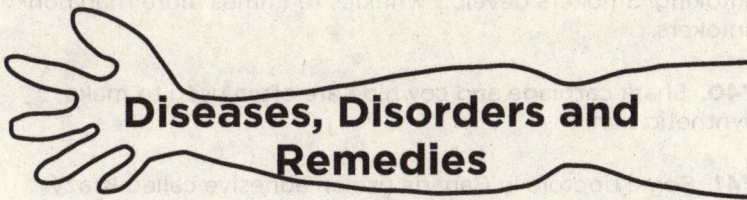

Diseases, Disorders and Remedies

731. Leprosy is the oldest known disease in the world.

732. Trichotillomania is a disorder characterized by an overwhelming urge to pull out one's own hair.

733. Exploding head syndrome is a rare disorder in which the sufferer hears a loud noise that seems to originate from his or her own head. This usually happens while they are sleeping.

734. Have you ever seen people without eyelashes or eyebrows? The condition is called madarosis.

735. Can't remember the precise word for something? Then you suffer from lethologica.

736. People who suffer from prosopagnosia, or face blindness, cannot recognize faces.

737. Imagine risking death every time you brush your hair! A teenage girl in Scotland has been found to suffer from a disorder called 'hair brushing syndrome'. The static electricity that is generated while she brushes her hair can cause her brain to shut down. To get around this, she has to let her hair hang on the side of her bed and brush it only when it is damp!

738. Persistent bad breath is called chronic halitosis. More than half the world's population suffers from this.

739. A simple tip to avoid developing wrinkles is to just stop smoking! Smokers develop wrinkles ten times more than non-smokers.

740. Shark cartilage and cowhide are often used to make synthetic skin.

741. Some doctors in Canada use an adhesive called Krazy Glue and other similar substances instead of stitches to minimize bacterial infection and scarring.

742. Aspirin was developed in 1897. In 1950, it became the highest selling drug in the world!

743. Do you know that aspirin was the first drug to be sold in tablet form?

744. Pez Mint dispensers were introduced in the market as an alternative to smoking.

745. Want to maintain healthy bones while enjoying a relaxing hobby? Head outside and try your hand at gardening. It's believed to be the best exercise to develop healthy bones!

746. Do you notice a greenish tinge in your hair after swimming? The chlorine content in the water is responsible for this. The remedy is quite simple. Pour ketchup on your wet hair, leave it for a couple of minutes and wash it. The red tone of the ketchup will neutralize the green and make it look beautiful.

747. Do you want to stay happy? The simplest natural remedy is to eat bananas! Serotonin, the hormone that makes us happy and cheerful is made from a protein called tryptophan, and banana is rich in it.

WEIRD
AND
WONDERFUL
PEOPLE

748

Did you know that Charlie Chaplin was the highest paid actor in his time? In 1916, he was earning about $10,000 on a weekly basis!

Politics

749. None of the US presidents was an only child.

750. Out of the first 44 presidents of the United States, 29 were of Irish descent. In fact, Barack Obama also belongs to this list.

751. What will you do if you become the president of your nation for just one day? This happened to David Rice Atchinson, the 12th president of the US, when James K. Polk stepped down from his post on 4 March 1849. Zachary Taylor, the next president, refused to be sworn in on a Sunday as it was the Sabbath and hence, David Rice Atchinson filled in for that 24-hour period!

752. During his 47 years of government service, Herbert Hoover, the 31st president of the US, donated all his salary to charity!

753. Andrew Johnson, the 17th president of the United States, could not read until he was 17 years old!

754. Martha Washington, the wife of George Washington, is the only woman to have appeared on the US paper currency. She was known as 'Lady Washington' and was given the title of 'First Lady of the United States' posthumously.

755. John F. Kennedy is the only US president to have won a Pulitzer Prize. It was for his work *Profiles in Courage*.

756. Mao Zedong never bathed or brushed his teeth in his entire life! He would only wash his mouth with tea.

757. Adolf Hitler actually wanted to be an architect. However, he couldn't achieve this dream because he failed the entrance exam!

Music

758. None of the members of the Beatles, the famous English rock band, knew how to read music! Paul McCartney learnt it out of his own interest.

759. Can you imagine a half-eaten French toast being sold on eBay for a price? Justin Timberlake's was!

760. Mozart, the prolific composer, could learn a piece of music in less than 30 minutes when he was just about four years old. This is when most of us just get comfortable talking. He started composing his own music at the age of five, when most of us just about start writing!

761. The Gloucestershire Airport in England would blast out Tina Turner's songs to scare birds away from the runways.

762. Mel Blanc, the American voice-over artist who was the voice of the famous Bugs Bunny, was allergic to carrots!

763. Mike Myers, the voice of Shrek in the *Shrek* series, picked up the accent he adopted for the movies from the one his mother put on while telling him bedtime stories when he was a child.

764. The popular American singer Paula Abdul used to be a cheerleader for the Los Angeles Lakers.

765. A man named Paul Mawhinney is known to have the world's largest album collection, with over 3 million music records, which he started collecting since the age of 12! These records are now safely kept in a warehouse almost 1,60,000 feet in size! Paul's collection of rare singles, unreleased records and others are worth over 50 million dollars!

766. Do think of the Australian opera singer Dame Nellie Melba when you enjoy your next Melba toast. After all, it's named after her!

767. Did you know that the music group 'Simply Red' got their name from a band member—Mick Hucknall—who had red hair?

Sports

768. Maria Spelterini, a professional tightrope walker, is the only woman to have crossed the Niagara Falls on high wire. She did it multiple times—once by wearing peach baskets that were strapped to her feet and then again blindfolded and then once more with her wrists and ankles manacled!

769. O.J. Simpson, the professional football player, suffered from rickets and wore leg braces in his childhood.

770. How many hands do you need to pin down an opponent? Morihei Ueshiba, the founder of aikido, once did it with just one finger!

771. Imagine jumping out of a plane without a parachute from an altitude of more than 21,000 m! A Russian named I.M. Chisov dared to take this plunge. He landed on a snow-covered mountain only to suffer a slight concussion and a fractured pelvis.

772. Lagarijo was a famous bullfighter in the 19th century. He killed more than 4850 bulls during his career.

The Motley Crew

773. How many times can one get married in a lifetime? For Linda Wolfe, the scope is quite high. She married 23 men and each of her marriages ended in a divorce or death of her spouse.

774. How many children can one father during a lifetime? Well, Rameses II, an Egyptian pharaoh, managed to father 156 children including 60 daughters and 96 sons! Wonder if he managed to remember all their names though!

775. How many children can a woman give birth to in a lifetime? The wife of Feodor Vassilyev, a Russian peasant, conceived 27 times and gave birth to a total of 69 children including 16 pairs of twins, four quadruplets and seven triplets, all within just 40 years (1725–1765)!

776. Do you travel light? Well, even if you travel with a lot of luggage, we bet you can't match Abdul Kassam Ismael, who was the Grand Vizier of Persia in the 10th century. He carried his entire library, consisting of 1,17,000 volumes loaded on 400 camels, wherever he went! We wonder how many of those books he actually read during his travel!

777. The name of Bill Gates may be synonymous with Microsoft but his posh house was designed using a Macintosh computer, manufactured by his rival company, Apple!

778. Darwin spent 39 years of his life studying only earthworms!

779. Dennis Easterling (from Atlanta, Georgia) rocked incessantly for 480 hours in a rocking chair. It is not very surprising that he holds the world record for this feat, isn't it?

780. Thomas Edison, who holds more than a 1000 patents in his name, once designed a helicopter that worked with gunpowder. Ironically, his own invention blew up his factory!

781. Did you know that Edison, who invented the light bulb, was afraid of the dark?

782. Though he invented the telephone, Alexander Graham Bell could never call up his mother or wife. They were both deaf.

783. Steve Fletcher collects gum wrappers from across the world and has a collection of more than 5300 wrappers, one of the largest collections owned by an individual.

784. Charles Osborne, an American farmer from Iowa, holds the Guinness World Record for having the longest hiccups. They persisted for more than 60 years! According to the doctors, a part of the brain stem that inhibits hiccups response was damaged and that had resulted in this prolonged suffering. In spite of this limitation, Osborne lived a normal life, married twice and fathered eight children! He was invited to many popular TV and radio shows, one of which was Robert Ripley's *Believe It or Not*.

785. GI Joe, Star Wars and He-Man rocked the action toy charts at one point of time. Do you know which series dominates the charts now? They are the action figures of famous contemporary personalities like Osama bin Laden, Tony Blair, President George W. Bush, Rudolph Giuliani—all of whom were tied to the tragic WTC attacks of September 2011. This peculiar collection, manufactured by Herobuilders, a toymaker in Connecticut, was an instant hit among toy collectors.

786. Rev. Dr Kevin Fast, a Canadian, lifted an 8' x 3' platform once. What's so special about that, you ask? Well, just that it was loaded with 20 women and he lifted the platform using just his back and legs!

787. Have you ever bought wall clocks and sculptures made of cow manure? Well, the magical hands of Bernd Eilts, a German artist, could turn dried cow manure into exotic decorative items! In fact, he is exploring ways of making watches out of this! Dung watches, anyone?

788. Have you ever wondered how strong human teeth can be? Belgium's John Massis put his teeth to test when he pulled a couple of New York Long Island railroad passenger cars with a thick rope, using just his teeth!

789. William James Sidis could speak eight languages when he was just eight years old. He had also written four books by then. He was considered the smartest person during his time. Geniuses generally have an IQ of more than 140. William's IQ was around 250 to 300, nearly double of a genius IQ. What's more, he went to Harvard Business School at 11!

790. Albert Einstein was not only a great scientist, but also a philanthropist. He would charge people for his autographs and speeches and then donate the proceeds to charity.

791. We all know Leonardo da Vinci was one of the most famous painters and sculptors of the Renaissance period. But did you know that he also invented scissors?

792. Do you know that Leonardo da Vinci was dyslexic? Due to this disorder he often wrote backwards!

SCIENCE, MATHS AND TECHNOLOGY

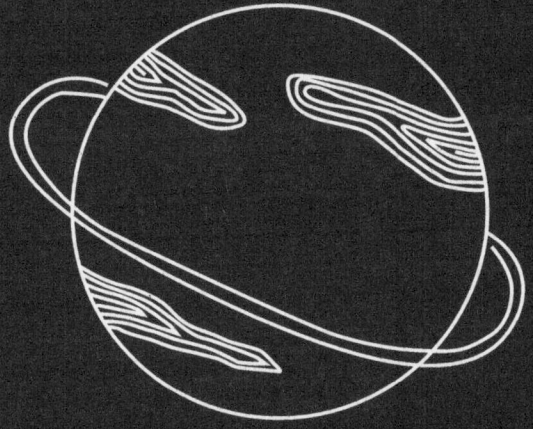

793

The earth becomes a few tons heavier every day! The meteoric dust from space that constantly accumulates on the earth's surface is increasing the weight of the planet steadily. Now, is there anyone who can suggest a 'weight loss' plan for our planet?

794. Did you know that hydrogen is the least dense substance in the world? It's also the most common atom found in the universe.

795. Check for missing letters in Mendeleev's Modern Periodic Table of the elements. You'll notice that the letter 'j' does not appear anywhere.

796. Do all rocks submerge in water? If your answer is yes, try dropping a pumice stone in it and see.

797. What is so special about minus 40 degrees Celsius and minus 40 Fahrenheit? Their values are the same.

798. When a liquid moves freely into outer space, what form does it take? It will naturally assume the form of a sphere due to surface tension.

799. Pyrite or iron disulfide looks very similar to gold. No wonder it is called 'fool's gold'!

800. Do you know that nylon, a synthetic fibre, is made from fossil fuels (petroleum and coal)?

801. Natural gas does not have an odour of its own. The strange odour that one can smell due to gas leak from an LPG cylinder is actually added by gas companies.

802. The year 2001 saw a breakthrough in the field of genetic engineering. This was the year the first genetically-engineered babies were born!

Eureka!

803. The rocking chair, the writing chair, the library step stool, the mechanical arm, the odometer, 'whale oil' candles and bifocal spectacles all have one factor in common—the inventor Benjamin Franklin!

804. Fire escapes, windshield wipers and bulletproof vests were all invented by women.

805. The idea of a pet rock was conceived by Gary Dahl of California when he heard his friends complaining about their pets. He jokingly said that his pet was perfect as it was 'a rock'! It was easy to take care of, and didn't need to be groomed, bathed, fed or walked every day. More importantly, it would never be disobedient or sick. Furthermore, it would not die and leave you sad. As weird as it sounds, he took the idea seriously enough to draft a humorous 'instruction manual' about keeping rocks as actual pets. What's more, he sold over 1 million pet rocks in 1975 and eventually became a millionaire!

806. The famous water-displacing spray, WD-40, got its name because it took 40 attempts for it to be created successfully!

807. The inspiration to use squared spikes in Nike shoes to make them lighter came to Bill Bowerman (the co-founder of Nike) while staring at a waffle iron!

808. Do you know that the cigarette lighter was invented much before the modern friction matches? Well, the cigarette lighter was invented by the German chemist J.W. Dobereiner in the year 1816. However, the modern matches (which are lit

SCIENCE, MATHS AND TECHNOLOGY

by friction against a rough surface) were invented only in the year 1827 by the British chemist John Walker. In fact, John Walker thought it was too trivial an invention to patent it!

809. Once, when an engineer named Percy Spencer walked by a radar tube, he found that the chocolate bar in his pocket had melted. Further research was conducted on this, which led to the invention of a gadget that most modern kitchens can't do without—the microwave.

810. Initially, milk was distributed in bottles. But when John Van Wormer dropped a bottle of milk by accident one morning, his sheer annoyance at cleaning up the mess led to the invention of paper milk cartons. It revolutionized the process of milk distribution.

811. Cornflakes was invented by the Kellogg Brothers (Will Keith Kellogg and Dr John Harvey Kellogg) when they were developing a nutritional cereal for patients at a health resort.

812. The candy box was an idea developed by Richard Cadbury as early as the 1800s.

813. Do you know who invented the electric chair? No prizes for guessing that it was a dentist!

814. The first ballpoint pen was invented by a Hungarian named Ladislo Biro in the year 1938.

815. Though the process of canning food was developed in 1810, the tin-opener wasn't invented until 1870.

816. There are multi-purposes coffins available today which can double up as wine racks, picnic tables and so on, before they're put to their actual use.

817. A cook in China accidentally mixed charcoal, saltpetre and sulphur in his kitchen and compressed it in a bamboo tube which, of course, exploded! We are not sure whether he lost his job after that, but he contributed in a big way to the invention of fireworks!

818. Play-Doh was invented by Joseph McVicker and Noah McVicker. It was originally meant to be a wallpaper cleaner!

Wonders of the Universe

819. The Milky Way contains nearly 400 billion stars. Do you know that there are more than a 100 billion such galaxies (some of them larger than the Milky Way) that have trillions of stars?

820. Do you know that one 'galactic year', which is the time taken by our solar system to complete one revolution around the centre of the Milky Way, is close to 250 million earth years! Wonder how many 'galactic' revolutions have been completed so far!

821. After the sun and the moon, the brightest object in our solar system is the planet Venus.

822. All planets are named after pagan gods, except for earth.

823. All planets in the universe rotate anticlockwise except for Venus.

824. We know that Jupiter is the largest planet in the solar system. But do you know that Jupiter is larger than all other planets combined in the solar system? In fact, the magnetic field of Jupiter is so strong that it stretches over millions of miles into the solar system and the electrical activity is so intense that the planet powers billions of watts into the magnetic field of the earth every day! Jupiter completes one rotation in less than 10 hours, making it the fastest rotating planet in the solar system.

825. The density of Saturn, the second largest plant in the solar system, is so low (one-tenth of the earth's density) that it is capable of floating on water.

826. Neptune was the first planet to be discovered by mathematicians on the basis of theoretical calculations.

827. Do you know that Pluto is the only planet in our solar system which has not been visited or explored by a spacecraft? Guess what could be the length of a plutonian year. It is 248 earth years! This means that the planet takes two and a half earth centuries (a quarter of a millennium) to complete just one revolution around the sun on its orbit!

828. Olympus Mons, on Mars, is the largest volcanic mountain in our entire solar system. It stretches to a width of 600 km and rises to a height of 27 km!

829. We all know that a planet has satellites and moons rotating around it. But do you know that a moon can have its own moon too? Scientists have found moons of three planets that have their own moons. They are Jupiter's Lo, Saturn's Titan and Neptune's Triton.

830. Do you know that footprints on the moon will last for millions of years? It's because the moon does not have an atmosphere.

831. Would you like to create a pathway to the moon and back? If all the cars in the US are lined up together bumper to bumper, this is achievable!

832. Why do binary stars dance around each other? It's because they are held together by the gravitational forces between each other.

833. Imagine a comet having more than a 300-million-km-long tail! This was the length of the tail of the Great Comet of 1843.

834. Did you know that Halley's Comet makes an appearance every 75 years? The last appearance was in February 1986. Next predicted date, July 2061.

835. There is a special relationship between Mark Twain and Halley's Comet. Mark Twain's birth and death, both took place on the day the earth saw Halley's Comet. In fact, he had predicted that the comet was going to be seen on the day of his death!

836. Asteroids have other asteroids revolving around them!

837. The only part of a space shuttle that is not painted is the external tank. This is because it is discarded after the launch. Do you know why the rest of the parts are painted? It is to prevent metal corrosion.

838. We send expensive spaceships to collect sample rocks from other planets. But do you know that some of the rocks found on earth are pieces from Mars or the moon?

839. Imagine having a post office at a space station! Yes, there is one at Mir, the Russian space station. The cosmonauts who visited the space station used unique postal 'markers' to stamp the envelopes.

840. Jan Davis and Mark Lee became the first and only couple to fly to space in September 1992!

841. Did you know that Valentina Tereshkova was the first woman to spend three days in space and successfully complete 48 orbits around the earth?

842. Humans aren't the only ones who've gone to space. The United States sent three mice into space in 1958. The mice were called Mia, Laska and Benji.

843. Did you know that a space shuttle named Discovery took along 32 fertilized chicken eggs into the orbit in 1989? The astronauts ate a wholesome Thanksgiving dinner consisting of turkey, cranberry sauce and gravy in their shuttle!

The Number Games

844. 28 is a perfect number because it is equal to the sum of all its positive divisors other than itself. (1+2+4+7+14=28). Can you find some other perfect numbers?

845. The number 2520 is quite special. It can be divisible by all numbers from 1 to 10.

846. Calculate 111,111,111 x 111,111,111. The answer is 12,345,678,987,654,321. All digits appear in ascending order from 1 to 9 and then again in descending order back to 1!

847. The value of Pi has been calculated to a precision of nearly 2,260,321,363 digits. The billionth digit of this number is 9.

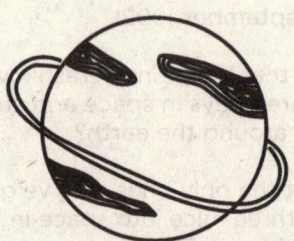

Saving the Environment

848. The ozone hole found in the Antarctic region in 1992 was found to be much larger than the North American continent.

849. At a time when fast racing cars compete for aggressive sales targets in the market, Netherlands encourages its citizens to cycle. More than 17,000 km of cycle lanes have been built so far. In fact, the city has special lanes and traffic lights just for cyclists.

850. There is a cruise liner named after Queen Elizabeth II. It moves only 6 inches for every gallon of diesel it burns.

851. Can you guess how much energy you can save by recycling? To give you an idea, you can save energy required to light a 100-Watt bulb for four hours by recycling just one glass bottle. Similarly, you can save energy required to run a television for three hours by recycling just one aluminium can.

852. Nearly 4 gallons of water are drained every minute into the gutter if you leave the water running while brushing your teeth.

853. Duracell, one of the leading manufacturers of batteries, reused the waste generated by the company to build some parts of its international headquarters.

854. Which is the largest manufacturing industry in the world? It is the automobile industry. In fact, automobiles are the most recycled product in the world! But surprisingly, statistics reveal that more steel is used to manufacture bottle caps than automobile bodies!

855. In order to complete one orbit around the earth, the Hubble telescope takes 97 minutes, during which it uses energy that can light up 30 household bulbs.

856. One gallon of used motor oil can pollute almost one million gallons of fresh water!

857. The next time your toaster is not in use, unplug it. Not many of us are aware that it will consume energy if it remains plugged.

858. Can you guess how many pounds of pollution a car produces on an average if you drive for 100 miles? Not less than 4 pounds, as with every 25 miles, there is a pound of pollution being hurled into the environment!

859. Just an acre of trees is enough to remove 13 tons of harmful gases and dust every year!

860. Did you know that 17 trees can actually absorb up to 250 pounds of carbon dioxide from air each year? You should also know that burning the same amount of paper made with these 17 trees would create more than 1500 pounds of carbon dioxide! Going forward, make a wise decision when it comes to paper—Save!

861. Did you know that a 15-year-old tree can be used to make only 700 paper bags?

862. Did you know that if we save all the amount of wood and paper that we otherwise throw away, we could produce enough power to heat 5,00,00, 000 homes for over 20 years?

863. Which appliance uses the most amount of water in your home? If you think it's the washing machine, you're wrong. It is the toilet!

864. Next time you see a leaking tap, make sure you get it fixed. A dripping tap can send 50 gallons of water to the drain, which is enough to run your dishwasher twice!

865. Cotton is one of the most widely used textile fibres in the world. But do you know that in order to protect a cotton crop, you need to spray pesticides at least 40 times a year?

866. Three African schoolgirls managed to invent a generator powered by urine in 2012. What an innovative way to nail alternate sources of energy!

867. Do you know that the use of chopsticks in China only, requires cutting down of 25 million trees annually?

868. The people of Weidenthal, South Germany, conduct a 'Knut-Fest' after Christmas. The competitors strip off the decorations and lights from Christmas trees and throw them in three different styles—high jump, javelin and hammer style. The person who throws them the farthest during the course of the day is the winner.

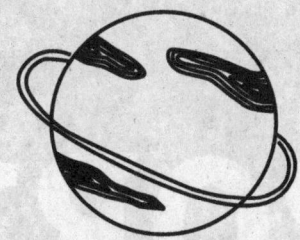

The World Wide Web

869. It took 38 years for radio to become popular and 13 years for television, whereas the Internet shot to popularity among 50 million users in just four years!

870. More than 350 million people in the world have access to computers. But half the world, consisting of a population of 6.5 billion people, hasn't even seen a telephone. Talk about unequal distribution of resources!

871. The first ever Internet domain to be registered was symbolics.com (1985).

872. Social networking sites have changed the lives of many across the world. According to a survey conducted in 2009, one out of eight married couples in the US met online!

873. Do you know what the word 'Google' means? It refers to the number 1 followed by a 100 zeros!

SPORTS
AND
GAMES

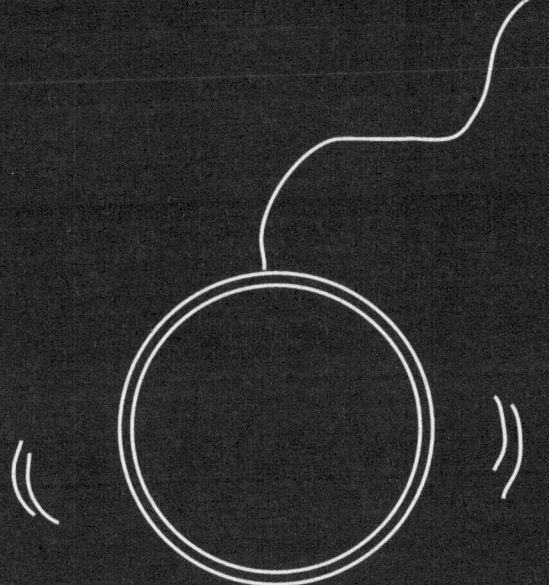

874

The 'yo-yo' was invented in the 16th century.
It was initially used as a weapon in the
Philippine Islands.

875. Once, a few boys who wanted to play rackets started knocking a ball around in a confined area adjacent to the court, while waiting for their turn. The game evolved into what we now know as squash.

876. Baseball players are not very likely to lend their bats to anyone. They believe it would jinx them!

877. Baseball caps were initially made of straw.

878. Most of us know that there are 64 squares (8 x 8) on a chessboard. Do you know how many squares there are on a Scrabble board? 255 (15 x 15).

879. In the world ice hockey championships, Canada beat Denmark (47-0) in the year 1949. This stupendous victory was surpassed by Australia in 1987 when the were victorious against New Zealand (58-0)!

880. In a 1912 Stockholm wrestling match, Finn Alfred Asikainen and Russian Martin Klien wrestled for over 11 hours! The winner, Klein, though, could not participate in the championship match as he was too exhausted.

881. Hockey pucks were made of frozen cow dung originally.

882. Scrabble, the popular board game of words, was invented by Alfred Butts. It was initially called Criss-Cross Words.

883. Kite-flying is a professional sport in Thailand.

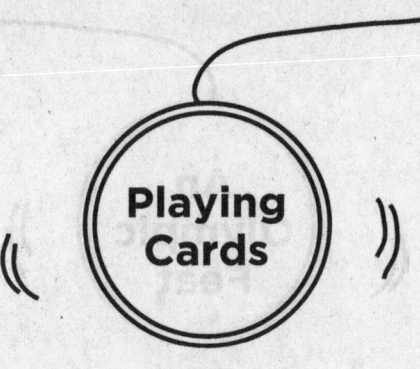

Playing Cards

884

- Playing cards were used as currency in France, in 1685, when there was a shortage of coins.
- Each of the kings in a deck of cards represents a great king from history. King of Spades – King David; King of Diamonds – Julius Caesar; King of Clubs – Alexander the Great; King of Hearts – Charlemagne.
- Only one of these kings is without a moustache. The King of Hearts!

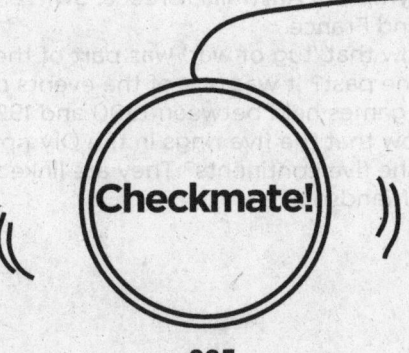

Checkmate!

885

- Chess originated in India.
- There are 3,18,97,95,64,000 ways of making the first four moves per side!
- The Persian phrase 'shah mat', which means 'the king is dead', is popularly known today in the context of chess as 'checkmate'.

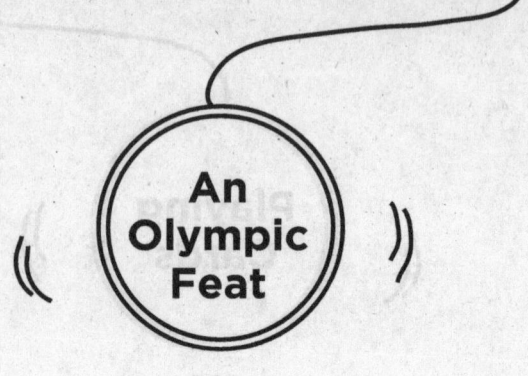

An Olympic Feat

886

- There was only one event in the first Olympic Games—foot race.
- The Olympic Flame was first introduced in the modern Olympics Games in the year 1928 in Amsterdam. Can you believe that in Ancient Greece, the mother flame that was used to light the Olympic torch was lit by the sun itself? A parabolic mirror was used to reflect the sun's rays and create the fire. Hence, the fire was considered to be pure. Since 1896, five countries have always participated in the modern Olympics—Australia, Greece, Switzerland, United Kingdom and France.
- Do you know that 'tug of war' was part of the Olympic Games in the past? It was one of the events conducted during the games held between 1900 and 1920.
- Do you know that the five rings in the Olympic symbol represent the five continents? They are linked together to symbolize friendship.

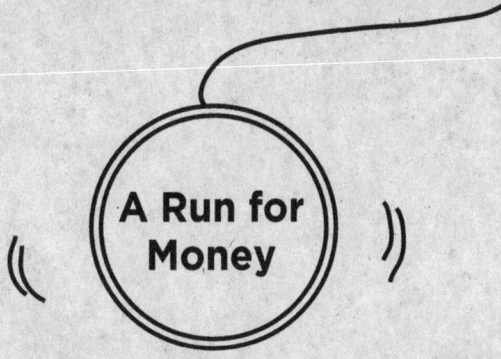

A Run for Money

887

- The game of monopoly was introduced in the year 1935.
- More than 200 million boards have been sold worldwide so far.
- 500 million people have played the game at least once.
- Monopoly has been even played underwater. The longest game to be played underwater was for 45 days!

Golfing Around

888

- Do you know that golf balls were initially made of wood, and then out of leather with stuffed feathers?
- Modern golf balls have dimples in them in order to make them go farther. The standard number of dimples on a regulation golf ball is 336.
- Can you believe that Tiger Woods, the professional golfer, was introduced to the game by his father, when Tiger was hardly nine months old?

LANGUAGE
AND
LITERATURE

889

Try reading this word:
Pneumonoultramicroscopicsilicovolcanokoniosis.
Consisting of 45 characters, this is the longest
English word listed in the official English dictionary.
It is a type of disease caused due to the
inhalation of fine silica dust particles that results in
the inflammation of lungs.

890. Languages have been in existence since 1,00,000 BCE! More than 6900 languages are spoken around the world today.

891. The number of official languages in a country differs from the number of living languages (which certain groups of people speak). Can you believe that though there are only three official languages recognized in Papua, New Guinea, there are more than 800 living languages spoken by the locals? India has around 20 official languages, but the number of *living* languages in the country, spoken in various regions, is no less than 400!

892. The language with the largest number of native speakers in the world is Mandarin Chinese. But do you know that both Hindi and Bengali are in the list of the top 10 languages with the largest number of native speakers? And if you look at the top 30 languages in this category, more than 10 are Indian languages!

893. All Japanese words that do not end with a vowel end with the letter 'n'!

894. How fast can you say this phrase—'the sixth sick sheik's sixth sheep's sick'? This is the most challenging tongue twister in English.

895. What is so special about the letter 'P' in the Roman alphabet? It is the only capital letter with just one end point.

896. Write the word CHOICE COD on a piece of paper and hold it front of the mirror upside down. You will observe that the words read the same!

897. Read the following sentence: Aoccdrnig to a rscheearch procejt at Cmabrigde Uinervtisy, it deosnt mttaer waht oredr the ltteers in a wrod are, the olny iprmoatnt tihng is taht the frist and lsat ltteer be in the rghit pclae. Tihs is bcuseae the huamn mnid deos not raed ervey lteter.

898. When you search for a new font on the web and want to see how the letters look, the most common sentence that is used for displaying the font is: 'The quick brown fox jumps over the lazy dog'. Do you know why? This sentence uses every letter in the English alphabet! The shortest English sentence that includes all the letters of the English language is 'Jackdaws love my big sphinx of quartz'.

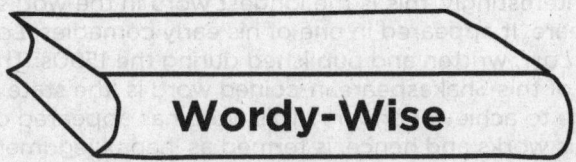

Wordy-Wise

899. Which language has the most number of words? English, of course! There are more than 2,50,000 distinct words in English. But can you believe that a language called Taki, spoken in certain regions of French Guinea, consists of just 340 words?

900. English is the language spoken by the largest number of non-native speakers around the world! There are nearly 350 million English speakers worldwide. In fact, due to its popularity, it is also the most widely published language.

901. Some English words are quite misleading. Here are some classic examples. 'Jackrabbits' are not rabbits. They are a certain species of hares with long ears and long hind legs and are found in parts of North America. A 'Jerusalem artichoke' is a type of sunflower. **Chinese ink** (Indian ink) was not known to India or China until recently. **Panama hats** do not come from Panama. They are made in Ecuador. The list goes on and on . . .

902. Do you know that more English speakers live in China than in the United States?

903. The most stolen book in public libraries is the *Guinness Book of World Records.* This is one of the records mentioned in the book!

904. The novel *Gadsby*, by Ernest Vincent Wright, which has about 50,000 words, does not contain the letter 'e'. This means that common words like 'the', certain plurals (ending with 'es'), past tense forms (ending with 'ed') and even abbreviations were not used!

905. 'Aladdin was a little Chinese boy'—This is how the original version of the *Tales of 1001 Arabian Nights* begins!

906. Read the word 'Honorificabilitudinitatibus' and observe the pattern of the letters. It has alternating consonants and vowels. Interestingly, this is the longest word in the works of Shakespeare. It appeared in one of his early comedies, *Love's Labour's Lost*, written and published during the 1590s. The meaning of this Shakespearean-coined word is 'the state of being able to achieve honours'. This word has appeared only once in his works and hence, is termed as 'hapax legomenon' (translated in Greek as 'occurring only once').

907. The Bible had over 40 authors, from all walks of life, including shepherds, farmers, tent-makers, physicians, priests, philosophers and kings, who wrote it over some 1500 years. The word 'Christian' occurs only three times in the entire text!

908. Can you believe that only 50 different words have been used to write an entire book? If you think this is impossible, read *Green Eggs and Ham*, a beginner's book written by Dr Seuss!

909. In 1990, two school districts in California banned the story *Little Red Riding Hood*, because the book had a picture of a basket with a wine bottle in it!

910. The shortest sentence in the English language that is considered complete is 'Go'.

911. What is the most commonly used word in a typical English conversation? The word 'I'.

912. How long is the phrase 'nineteen letters long'? It is actually 19 letters long!

913. Can you think of an English word with three consecutive sets of repetitive letters? It is 'bookkeeper' (o, k, e are repeated).

914. Two letters do not occur in the spelling of any cardinal number—'j' and 'k'!

915. Month, purple, silver and orange—these four common words do not rhyme with any other words in the English language.

916. What is the dot over the letters 'i' and 'j' called? A tittle.

917. Do you know what the # key on your keyboard is called? An octothorp.

918. Observe the words 'facetious' and 'abstemious'. These are the only two words in English in which the vowels are in alphabetical order—a,e,i,o,u.

919. Do you know what the act of snapping one's fingers is called? Fillip.

920. We use dice for a number of board games. But do you know what the dots or markings on the dice are called? They are called 'pips'.

921. Have you heard of the terms 'loonie' and 'toonie'? The $1 coin in Canada is called a loonie as it has a picture of a loon. The $2 coin is named 'toonie' as it is equivalent to two loonies.

922. The little dots of paper that fall out when you punch a hole in a sheet of paper using a puncher are referred to as 'chad'.

923. The crescent-shaped white part at the bottom of your fingernails is called the 'lunula' as it looks like a half moon (luna means 'of the moon').

924. Do you find it hard to get out of bed in the mornings? The state is called 'dysania'.

925. Have you heard of the term 'quinquennium'? It refers to a period of five years.

926. The stringy substance in an egg white is called a 'chalaza'.

927. The tiny plastic tubes at the end of your shoelaces are called 'aglets'.

928. Do you have a gap between your teeth? The term used to refer to this gap is 'diastema'. It is considered lucky in many countries, including France, Australia, Namibia, Ghana and Nigeria. It's also considered to be one of the seven signs of beauty in Netherlands.

929. Type the word TYPEWRITER on your keyboard. Do you observe anything interesting about the typing pattern? Well, it is the longest word you can type using just one row of a keyboard.

930. Type the word 'STEWARDESSES' on your computer. It's the longest English word that can be typed only with the left hand.

931. Punctuation didn't exist before the 15th century!

Word History

932. Recipe: The word 'recipe' comes from the Latin verb *recipre*, meaning 'to receive'. It appears to have entered the English language in the 1400s. At that time, it was common for physicians to place the word (the second person singular imperative of the verb recipere) at the top of prescriptions, before listing the ingredients that the patient was to 'receive' for his or her medical remedy. Amazingly, the first citation for the word in relation to cookery appeared as late as 1716. Before the 1700s, the everyday word for a culinary recipe was 'receipt'.

933. Hat Trick: During the 1850s, a bowler who got three batsmen out in a row was presented with a new white hat. This gave rise to the expression 'hat trick'.

934. Limelight: Before the invention of electricity, during live theatre performances, lime was burned in a lamp, and this created a white light that was directed at the performers. Now you know where the word 'limelight' comes from!

935. Jeep: Do you know that the word 'jeep' originated from the abbreviation G.P., a term used in the army for 'General Purpose' vehicles?

936. Vaccination: Can you believe that the first vaccine was actually 'contaminated' with another virus? Smallpox, a deadly disease, killed many people during the 18th century. Edward Jenner, a British doctor, observed that milkmaids who caught the cowpox virus did not catch smallpox. He invented the first successful vaccine for smallpox that contained the strains of the cowpox virus. He, in fact, coined the word 'vaccination', which is derived from the Latin root 'vaccinus', and means of or from cows.

937. Dude: Oscar Wilde and his friends put together parts of the words 'DUds' and 'attituDE' to create 'dude'! People have been using this word since the 1800s!

938. JUGGERNAUT: Derived from the Sanskrit 'Jagannath', one of the names of the god Krishna, this word denotes a ruthless, unbeatable force (literally or figuratively) in colloquial English.

939. Siamese Twins: One of the earliest known conjoined twins, Chang and Eng Bunker, were born in Siam (now Thailand) in 1811. They moved to America, exhibited themselves to make money, married sisters and had 10 and 11 children respectively! The twins met an unfortunate death, when one brother died of pneumonia and the other brother died soon after that, as he didn't want the doctor to separate him from his twin.

940. Mantelpiece: In the olden days, people would hang their coats, which were also called 'mantles', over the fireplace to dry them. That's how the framework above a fireplace came to be known as a 'mantelpiece'.

LANGUAGE AND LITERATURE

MIXED BAG

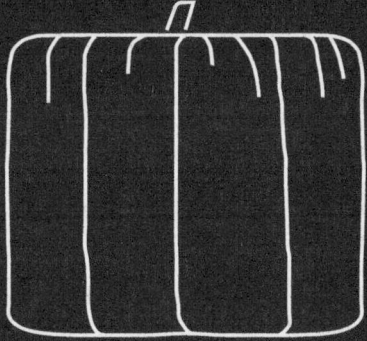

941

Japan has square watermelons!
This helps them stack and use space in a
better manner.

942. Where can you find the most number of Rolls Royce cars in the world? Hong Kong.

943. Russia has the largest number of movie theatres in the world.

944. Which was the first ship to use the SOS signal? The *Titanic*. It took 7 million dollars to build the ship and about 200 million to make a movie on it.

945. Diamonds are the hardest natural substances present in the earth. The word 'diamond' originated from the Greek word 'adamas' which means 'not conquerable'.

946. The first ever product to get its barcode scanned was a packet of Wrigley's chewing gum!

947. Tootsie Roll, one of the first brands to sell individually wrapped penny candies, manufactures around 16 million lollipops in just one day!

948. The most popular first name in the world is Muhammad and the most popular name used in nursery rhymes is Jack! Now, how many rhymes do you know with Jack as one of its characters?

949. Would you pay $71,380 for a 4-inch perfume bottle? A bottle of Parfum VI, made by Arthur Burnham, costs that much. And why wouldn't it? It's covered with 24-carat gold and diamonds!

950. Do you know that Iceland consumes more Coca-Cola than any other nation?

951. McDonald's is quite happy with their Happy Meals. They make about 40 per cent of their profits only through the sale of their Happy Meals!

952. Ladybugs are considered to be good luck charms around the world!

953. Warner Communications holds the copyright of the evergreen 'Happy Birthday' song and earns an annual revenue of about $2 million!

954. The Mayans used cacao beans as currency!

955. Jack-o'-lanterns were originally made out of turnips or potatoes.

956. Do you know that about 5,00,000 earthquakes are detected every year? But not all of them cause disastrous consequences as their intensities vary largely.

957. Guess how many cloud droplets make up just a single raindrop. Not less than a million!

958. The chihuahua is native to Mexico. In fact, it is named after a Mexican state.

959. Ancient civilizations considered comets to be signs of doom and disaster.

960. How many companies do you think can make more than a $16,000 revenue in their very first year? If you read the Microsoft story, you would know how they did it!

961. Did you know that Mastercard was originally known as Mastercharge? This form of payment came into being in 1976 when 14 banks merged to form a powerful credit card.

962. Coffee houses have proved to be lucky charms for powerful businesses. Lloyds of London was initially Lloyd's Coffee House. The East India Company, similarly, was originally Jerusalem Cafe. The Baltic Coffee House went on to become the London Shipping Exchange. In fact, New York Stock Exchange was initially a coffee house too!

963. Try folding a standard size paper in half. How many times can you do that? We bet you can't do it more than seven times.

964. Can you guess the duration of the shortest commercial flight between two continents? Covering a distance of 34 miles, the flight is between Gibraltar (Europe) and Tangier (Africa), and takes just 20 minutes!

965. One drop of seawater contains about a billion gold atoms!

966. About 97 per cent of the water on earth comes from the oceans and seas and is unsafe to drink.

967. The famous English writer Charles Dickens had a pet raven named Grip.

968. Want your rubber bands to last longer? Store them in the refrigerator.

969. How do mosquito repellents work? They don't exactly repel mosquitoes. They hide you from them. The spray blocks their sensors and so the mosquitoes are not aware of your presence.

970. Yen Sid, the sorcerer in the Disney film *Fantasia*, is actually Disney spelt backwards!

971. Colgate faced a big problem selling their brand in Spanish-speaking countries, because the word 'colgate' translates to the phrase 'Go hang yourself'!

972. If you board a flight from Tokyo at 7 in the morning to Honolulu, you would reach your destination at 4:30 p.m. the previous day. Who says time travel isn't possible?

973. Hold a seashell to your ear. Can you hear the sound of the sea? Contrary to popular belief, the sound doesn't originate from the shell. It is caused by the echo of blood pulsing in your ear.

974. Oreo, the world's best loved cookie, celebrated its 100th birthday last year!

998. What is the first word you write when somebody gives you a new pen? 97 per cent of the people write their own names.

999. Germany has been often referred to as the 'land of poets and thinkers'.

1000. If you take the net worth of the three wealthiest families in the world, you'll find that they possess more assets than 48 of the poorest nations combined!